# Welcome to
# Computers for
# ESL Students,
# 3rd Edition

**LOIS WOODEN**
Manteca Adult School

## LABYRINTH
LEARNING™

El Sobrante, CA

President:
Brian Favro

Product Development Manager:
Jason Favro

Managing Editor:
Laura Popelka

Production Manager:
Rad Proctor

eLearning Production Manager:
Arl S. Nadel

Editorial/Production Team:
Alona Harris, Silvia Mendez

Cover Design:
Huckdesign

*Welcome to Computers for ESL Students, 3rd Edition*
by Lois Wooden

ITEM:        1-59136-434-5
ISBN-13:  978-1-59136-434-4


Manufactured in the United States of America.

0 9 8 7 6 5 4 3 2

**Distributed By:**
**Grass Roots Press**
**Toll Free: 1-888-303-3213**
**Fax: (780) 413-6582**
**Web Site: www.grassrootsbooks.net**

# Table of Contents

# Preface

*Welcome to Computers for ESL Students, 3rd Edition* takes students with at least a Low Intermediate ESL reading proficiency (as defined by the CASAS Skill Level Descriptors for ESL) through the basics of effectively using a computer to perform basic tasks. Using a highly visual approach combined with a wealth of individual and paired exercises, this book introduces students to the beginning-level skills of using computers that run Windows 7. This third edition includes coverage of Word 2010 and all new WebSims.

**Learning Objectives:** The global learning objective for this textbook is qualified by each student's reading level upon enrollment in the course. After completing this course, students with a High Intermediate or above reading level should be able to study in a traditional beginner level course. Students with a Low Intermediate or below reading level should be able to continue learning using more advanced instructor-led lessons.

**About the Workbook:** An affordable workbook is available to complement this textbook. Students write directly in the workbook as they complete various individual and paired learning activities. It is highly recommended that each student have a copy of the workbook.

For almost two decades, Labyrinth Learning has been publishing easy-to-use textbooks that empower educators to teach complex subjects quickly and effectively, while enabling students to gain confidence, develop practical skills, and compete in a demanding job market. We add comprehensive support materials, assessment and learning management tools, and eLearning components to create true learning solutions for a wide variety of instructor-led, self-paced, and online courses.

Our textbooks follow the *Labyrinth Instructional Design,* our unique and proven approach that makes learning easy and effective for every learner. Our books begin with fundamental concepts and build through a systematic progression of exercises. Quick Reference Tables, precise callouts on screen captures, carefully selected illustrations, and minimal distraction combine to create a learning solution that is highly efficient and effective for both students and instructors.

This course is supported with *comprehensive instructor support* materials that include printable solution guides for side-by-side comparisons, test banks, customizable assessments, customizable PowerPoint presentations, detailed lesson plans, preformatted files for integration to leading learning management systems, and more. Our unique WebSims allow students to perform realistic exercises for tasks that cannot be performed in the computer lab.

## Visual Conventions

This book uses many visual and typographical cues to guide you through the lessons. This page provides examples and describes the functions of each cue.

**Type this text**

Anything you should type at the keyboard is printed in this typeface.

Command→
Command→
Command→etc.

This convention indicates how to give a command from the Ribbon. Commands are written Ribbon Tab→Command Group→Command→[subcommand].

This icon indicates the availability of a web-based simulation for an exercise or other online content. You may need to use a WebSim if your computer is not set up to support particular exercises.

Vocabulary sections introduce nouns and verbs used in the lesson.

Exercises provide hands-on experience with each concept.

Skill Builders provide additional hands-on practice with moderate assistance.

Paired Conversations provide oral practice of practical conversations that include computer vocabulary terms and phrases.

# Learning About Computer Basics

## LEARNING OBJECTIVES

After studying this lesson, you will be able to:

**Computer Objectives**

- Turn the computer on and off
- Identify the major parts of the computer
- Use the mouse

**Language Objectives**

- Use vocabulary words to describe parts of the computer
- Use computer verbs to describe actions
- Talk with a partner about the computer

*Student Resources **labyrinthelab.com/esl3***

# Vocabulary

## Picture Dictionary – Nouns

A noun is the name of a person, place, or thing. The following nouns are introduced in this lesson:

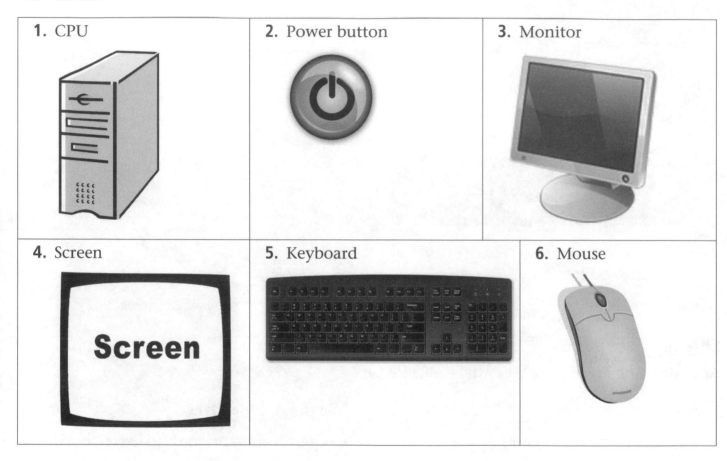

1. CPU

2. Power button

3. Monitor

4. Screen

5. Keyboard

6. Mouse

1. **CPU (Central Processing Unit)** – The brain of the computer system

2. **Power button** – The button that turns the computer on

3. **Monitor** – The part of the computer that you look at to see your work; like a television

4. **Screen** – The part of the monitor that lights up and shows what is happening on the computer

5. **Keyboard** – The part that you type on with all the letters, symbols, and functions

6. **Mouse** – The small oval piece that you can use to move from one part of the screen to another

# Picture Dictionary – Nouns (continued)

| 7. Mouse button | 8. Desktop | 9. Icon |
|---|---|---|
|  |  |  |

**7. Mouse button** – The top-left part at the top of the mouse that you use to control the mouse movement

**8. Desktop** – The first thing you see on your screen after you turn on the computer

**9. Icon** – A picture that represents a program or command

# Computer Verbs

A verb tells an action or what a subject is or does. The following verbs are introduced in this lesson:

| VERB | MEANING | EXAMPLE |
|------|---------|---------|
| **1.** Turn on | To give power to the computer so that it works | Please turn on the CPU and the monitor so that we can do our work. |

> ⚠️ **NOTE!**  Two-word verbs, like "turn on" can have different meanings from just one of the words, like "turn."

| VERB | MEANING | EXAMPLE |
|------|---------|---------|
| **2.** Turn off | To stop the power from going to the computer | I am finished with my work, so I can turn off the computer now. |
| **3.** Press | To push a button with your finger | If you want to turn on the computer, you have to press the power button. |
| **4.** Let go | To take your finger off the mouse button after you press it | When you use the mouse button, you have to press it and then let go. |
| **5.** Click | To press and let go of the mouse button (left side) in one smooth motion | Normally, you click the mouse button if you want to do something on the computer. |
| **6.** Go to | To take your mouse pointer to an icon or program name that you see on your screen | If you want to practice dragging, you can use the mouse to go to different icons and drag them on the screen. |
| **7.** Select | To choose a letter, word, sentence, paragraph, or program | I want to move that icon, so I will select and then drag it. |

| VERB | MEANING | EXAMPLE |
|------|---------|---------|
| **8.** Shut down | To turn off the computer using the Start menu | I am finished with my work, so I will shut down the computer. |
| **9.** Drag | To use your mouse to take something to a different position on the screen | I don't like that icon in that corner, so I will drag it to a different place. |

 **NOTE!**     In this lesson, the verb form "dragging" may be used instead of the verb form "drag."

# Concepts and Exercises

### CONCEPT 1.1 Computer Basics

Computers are an important part of life today. It is important to learn how to use them. Computers can be very useful at home and at work.

Here are some common things that you can learn to do with a computer:

- Apply for a job

- Type a personal or business letter

- Make a picture or graph

- Find maps and driving directions

- Find information that you need for school or work reports

- Send and receive mail, even from other countries

- Translate words

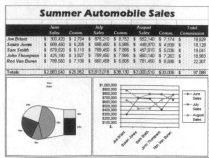

## CONCEPT 1.2 Parts of the Computer

Here are the parts of a computer system. Each one has its own special job.

A. **CPU** – The CPU (Central Processing Unit) is where all the "thinking" is done. Some people call it a tower. CPUs come in different shapes and sizes.

B. **Monitor** – The CPU uses the monitor to give you information. It shows you what the computer is doing.

C. **Speakers** – The speakers let you hear the sounds that the computer makes.

D. **Keyboard** – You use the keyboard to put numbers and letters into the computer.

E. **Mouse** – The mouse lets you point at and select different things on the computer screen.

 EXERCISE 1.2 **Find Computer Parts**

In this exercise, you will find the parts of the computer.

1. Sit down at a computer.

2. Look at the picture of the parts of the computer above. Find those parts on your computer.

## CONCEPT 1.3 The Correct Way to Sit at the Computer

It is important to sit correctly when using the computer so that your body will not hurt after using it.

**A.** Sit up straight in your chair.     **B.** Keep your wrists straight.

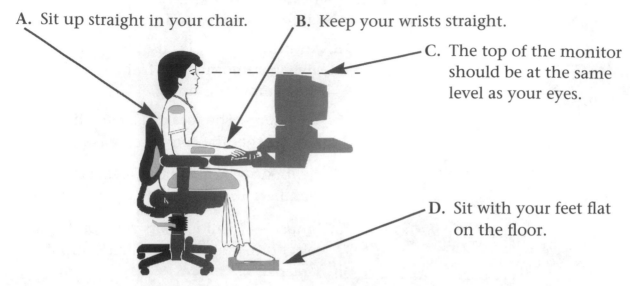

**C.** The top of the monitor should be at the same level as your eyes.

**D.** Sit with your feet flat on the floor.

The correct way to sit at a computer

 ## EXERCISE 1.3 Sit at the Computer Correctly

In this exercise, you will sit at the computer in the correct way.

1. Sit in a chair in front of a computer. Put your hands on the keyboard.

2. Ask your partner to check your sitting position. You should have your feet, back, wrists, and eyes in the correct positions.

## CONCEPT 1.4  Turning On the Computer

On the front of the CPU, you will see some slots and some buttons. Each one has a special job.

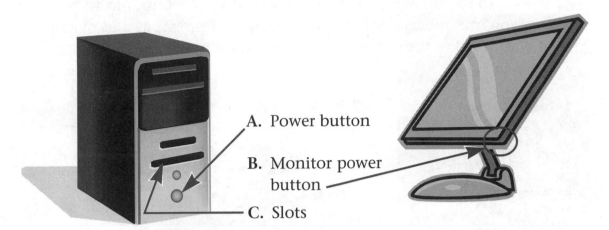

A. Power button

B. Monitor power button

C. Slots

To turn on the computer, press the CPU power button. To turn on the monitor, press the monitor power button.

 EXERCISE 1.4  **Turn On the Computer**

In this exercise, you will turn on the computer and monitor.

1. Push the **power button** on the CPU of a computer in your classroom.

2. Listen for the computer to turn on. You should hear a beep as it warms up.

3. Push the **power button** on the monitor to turn it on.

   Once the computer and monitor have been on for a few minutes, you should see the Windows Desktop.

**What Is Windows?**

Windows is a special program that you can use to communicate with the CPU. Windows must be put onto the computer before you can do anything on the computer. The CPU uses Windows to communicate in a language that you can understand. It also tells the other programs and machines that are attached to the computer, such as the printer, what to do.

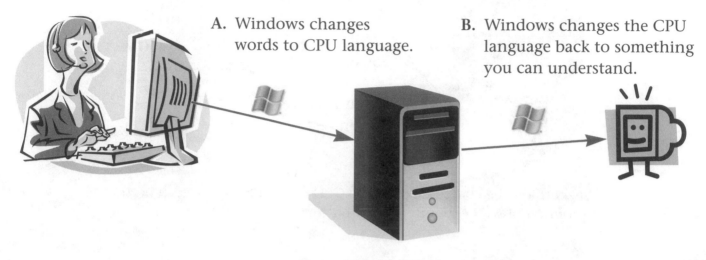

**A.** Windows changes words to CPU language.

**B.** Windows changes the CPU language back to something you can understand.

**EXERCISE 1.5** **Move the Mouse Pointer**

In this exercise, you will move the mouse on the Windows Desktop.

1. Look at the **Windows Desktop** on the screen. It should look similar to the next screen. (It may have a different picture on it or none at all.)

2. Move your mouse around and watch the **mouse pointer** (the small arrow) move on the screen.

 Mouse pointer

## CONCEPT 1.6  **Using a Mouse**

The mouse is used to point at things on the screen. It is called a mouse because the cord looks like a tail. Some mice come without cords and are called cordless mice.

When using the mouse, remember these tips:

- You usually use the left button of the mouse to click.

- If you need to use the right button, you will be told to right-click.

- The thumb and the fourth finger are used to hold the mouse and to help move it to new places.

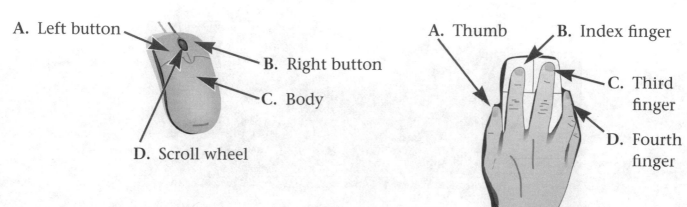

A. Left button
B. Right button
C. Body
D. Scroll wheel

A. Thumb
B. Index finger
C. Third finger
D. Fourth finger

**EXERCISE 1.6  Use the Mouse**

In this exercise, you will use the mouse.

1. Hold the sides of the mouse with your thumb and fourth finger. You should have one finger on each button. Do not hold it too tightly!

2. Put the bottom part of your hand on the mouse pad.

3. Move the mouse around and watch the mouse pointer move on the screen.

4. Move the mouse so the pointer is on top of one of the icons on the Desktop. Click (press and then let go) the left mouse button one time and see the color change on the icon.

   This is how the icon should look after you click on it.

5. Put your mouse on top of one of the icons. Hold down the left button and move the mouse. You should see the icon move to a new place when you let go. This is called dragging.

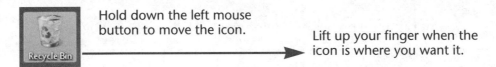
Hold down the left mouse button to move the icon.
Lift up your finger when the icon is where you want it.

6. Practice dragging icons to different parts of the Desktop.

## CONCEPT 1.7  Turning Off the Computer

To keep the computer working correctly, you must turn it off correctly.

Start→Shut down

This is an example of a command. When you give a command, you tell the computer to do something for you.

## EXERCISE 1.7  Turn Off the Computer

In this exercise, you will turn off the computer.

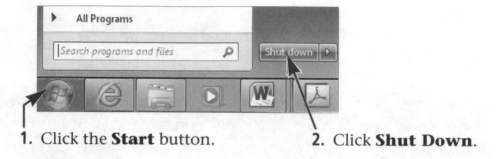

1. Click the **Start** button.

2. Click **Shut Down**.

Do not push the power button on the CPU. It will go off by itself.

# Skill Builder Exercises

**SKILL BUILDER 1.1**  ## Turn On the Computer

In this exercise, you will turn on the computer and monitor.

1. Press the **power button** on the CPU. Listen for the computer to beep.

2. Press the **power button** on the monitor.

---

**SKILL BUILDER 1.2**  ## Drag Icons

In this exercise, you will drag icons on the screen.

1. Use your mouse to drag all of the icons on the Desktop to the **bottom-right corner** of the screen.

2. Use your mouse to drag all of the icons on the Desktop to the **top-right corner** of the screen.

3. Use your mouse to drag all of the icons on the Desktop to the **left side** of the screen.

---

**SKILL BUILDER 1.3**  ## Turn Off the Computer

In this exercise, you will turn off the computer and monitor.

1. Click the **Start** button.

2. Click **Shut Down**.

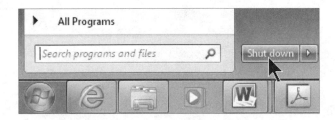

3. Press the **power button** on the monitor to turn it off.
Do not push the power button on the CPU. It will go off by itself.

---

**Personal Project: Describe Computer Parts**

In this exercise, you will describe the different parts of the computer.

1. On a piece of paper, make a list of five parts of a computer system.

2. Describe in your own words what each part looks like. Write one sentence about each part.

# Conversation

## Paired Conversation

With a partner, take turns reading the A and B parts of the conversation.

| | |
|---|---|
| Student A | Hi. What's that? |
| Student B | This is my new computer. |
| Student A | Really? How exciting! |
| Student B | Let me show you. This is the CPU. |
| Student A | I know. It's the brain. |
| Student B | That's right! This is the monitor. |
| Student A | Wow! It has a nice screen. |
| Student B | Yes, it helps me to see clearly what is happening on the computer. Look at my fancy keyboard. |
| Student A | I know about the keyboard. My brother takes keyboarding at school. |
| Student B | This is the mouse and these are the mouse buttons. The left one is used more often than the right. |
| Student A | What a cute mouse. Can I push a button? |
| Student B | No, not yet! You have to turn on the computer first. |
| Student A | Okay. Can I push the power button to turn it on now? |
| Student B | Sure. The first thing you see is the Desktop. |
| Student A | The screen looks colorful. |
| Student B | Thanks. I love my new computer! |
| Student A | You are so lucky! |

# Using Windows and the Start Menu

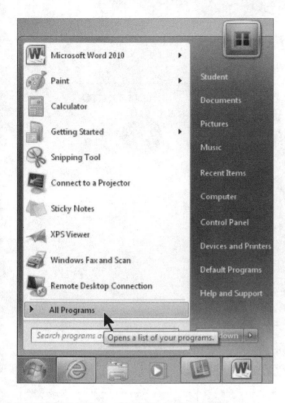

## LEARNING OBJECTIVES

After studying this lesson, you will be able to:

### Computer Objectives

- Identify the parts of a program window
- Use the Start menu to open a program
- Move a window using the mouse
- Minimize, maximize, restore, and close a window

### Language Objectives

- Talk with a partner about the different parts of a window
- Talk about how to find and use different buttons, bars, menus, and the Ribbon
- Describe how to move a window and use the sizing buttons

*Student Resources* **labyrinthelab.com/esl3**

 # Vocabulary

## Picture Dictionary – Nouns

A noun is the name of a person, place, or thing. The following nouns are introduced in this lesson:

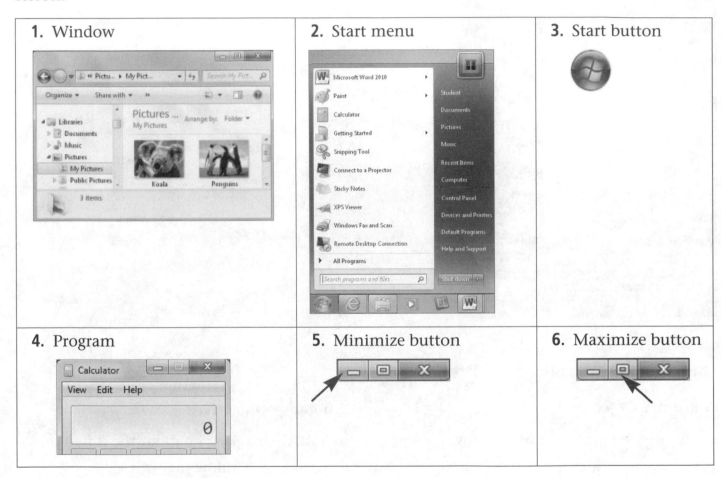

1. Window
2. Start menu
3. Start button
4. Program
5. Minimize button
6. Maximize button

1. **Window** – A rectangular area on the screen that shows a program or message

2. **Start menu** – The list that appears when you click on the Start button; it shows the main programs

3. **Start button** – The button on the bottom-left corner of your screen that opens the Start menu

4. **Program** – A set of directions (such as Microsoft Word, computer games, Calculator, and WordPad) that tells the computer what to do to get a job done

5. **Minimize button** – The button that looks like a minus sign at the top-right corner of a window; it makes the window disappear, but the program is still open

6. **Maximize button** – The square button between Minimize and Close that makes a window fill the whole screen

# Picture Dictionary – Nouns (continued)

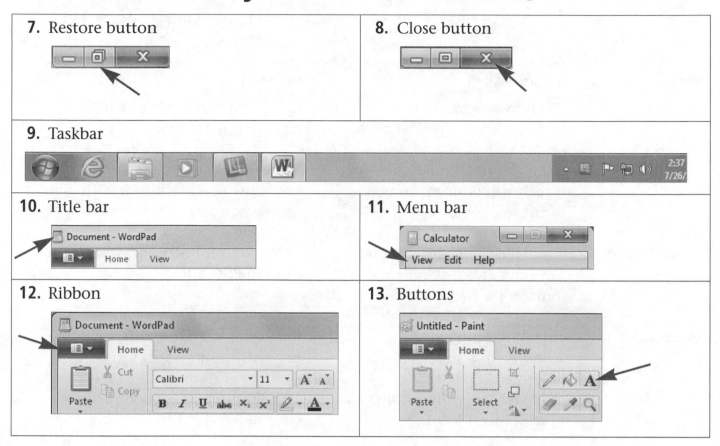

7. Restore button

8. Close button

9. Taskbar

10. Title bar

11. Menu bar

12. Ribbon

13. Buttons

7. **Restore button** – The button in the same place as Maximize that changes a large window to a smaller size

8. **Close button** – The button with an "X" that closes the window; it makes the window disappear and also closes the program

9. **Taskbar** – The bar at the bottom of the screen that shows all open programs

10. **Title bar** – The bar at the very top of a window that shows the name of the program you are using

11. **Menu bar** – The bar with words that is below the title bar and gives you ways to use the program

12. **Ribbon** – A bar showing different icons; each icon does a different job when you click on it

13. **Buttons** – Icons that do different things when you click them with the mouse

# Computer Verbs

A verb tells an action or what a subject is or does. The following verbs are introduced in this lesson:

| VERB | MEANING | EXAMPLE |
|---|---|---|
| 1. Open | To show a window | If you want to use WordPad, you have to open it first. |
| 2. Point | To make the mouse pointer touch something that you want to choose | When you want to select an icon, you must first point to it with your mouse pointer. |
| 3. Minimize | To make a window disappear (but not close) so only its button shows on the taskbar | I want to minimize this window so I can look at another window. |
| 4. Restore | To change a maximized window to a smaller size | I'm going to restore this window because I don't want it to be so big. |
| 5. Maximize | To make the window larger so that it fills the entire screen | I need to maximize my window because I want it to be as big as possible. |
| 6. Close | To stop a program and make it not show on your screen anymore | Class is finished. Please close your windows and turn off your computers. |

# Concepts and Exercises

CONCEPT 2.1 **The Windows Desktop**

The Windows Desktop appears when you turn on the computer. Sometimes it shows a picture. It has these main parts:

**A. Icons** – Pictures that represent programs or commands

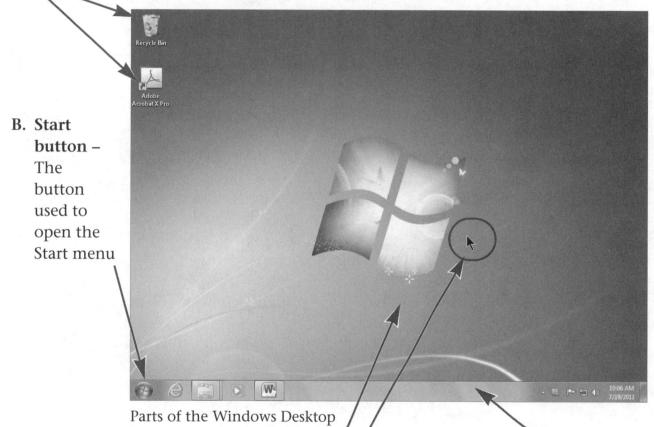

Parts of the Windows Desktop

**B. Start button** – The button used to open the Start menu

**C. Desktop** – The first thing you see when your computer is turned on and you have not opened any windows

**D. Mouse pointer** – A small object that moves on the screen when you move your mouse

**E. Taskbar** – The bar at the bottom of the screen that shows all open programs

EXERCISE 2.1 **Use the Windows Desktop**

In this exercise, you will use the Windows Desktop.

1. If necessary, turn on the computer.
   You should see the Windows Desktop on the screen.

2. Move your mouse and watch the mouse pointer move on the screen.

3. Point (don't click) with your mouse pointer over the **Recycle Bin**.

4. Point (don't click) with your mouse pointer over the **Start** button.

5. Point (don't click) with your mouse pointer over the **taskbar**.

## CONCEPT 2.2  Opening a Program

 You use the Start button to start programs with the Start menu. The Start menu shows the programs that the computer can run. The Start menu also allows you to do other things, such as turn off the computer.

## EXERCISE 2.2  Start the WordPad Program

In this exercise, you will use the Start button to start the WordPad program.

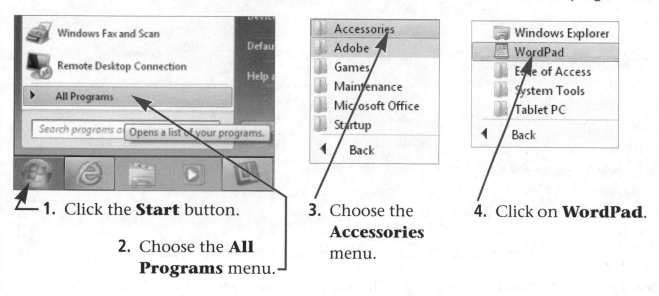

1. Click the **Start** button.

2. Choose the **All Programs** menu.

3. Choose the **Accessories** menu.

4. Click on **WordPad**.

5. Leave the WordPad window open.

## CONCEPT 2.3  Parts of a Program Window

Most program windows have parts similar to what you see on the screen in WordPad. Look at the picture below to identify the different parts of a program window.

**A. Title bar** – The title bar is always at the very top of the window. It tells you the name of the program you are using.

**B. Ribbon** – The Ribbon has different buttons that make different things happen when you click them with the mouse. You will learn more about it later.

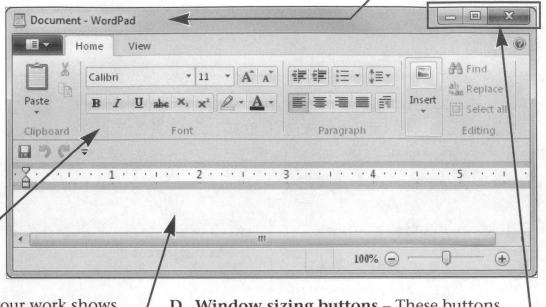

**C. Work area** – The work area is the place where your work shows when you put it into the computer by typing or using the mouse.

**D. Window sizing buttons** – These buttons control the size of the window.

# Window Sizing Buttons

Window sizing buttons can change the size of the program window, close it, or make it disappear from the screen without closing it.

**A. Minimize** – The Minimize button makes the window disappear when you click on it. The window is not closed, just hiding. You can see that window again if you click its button on the taskbar.

**B. Maximize** – When you click the Maximize button, it makes the window fill the whole screen.

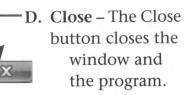

**D. Close** – The Close button closes the window and the program.

**C. Restore** – When you click the Restore button, the window returns to the size it had before it was maximized.

## EXERCISE 2.3  Work with WordPad

In this exercise, you will look at features of the WordPad program window and use the window sizing buttons.

**NOTE!** Do not click in steps 1–6; just point at parts of the WordPad window.

**1.** Put your mouse pointer on the **Ribbon** (don't click).

**2.** Put your mouse pointer on the **title bar**.

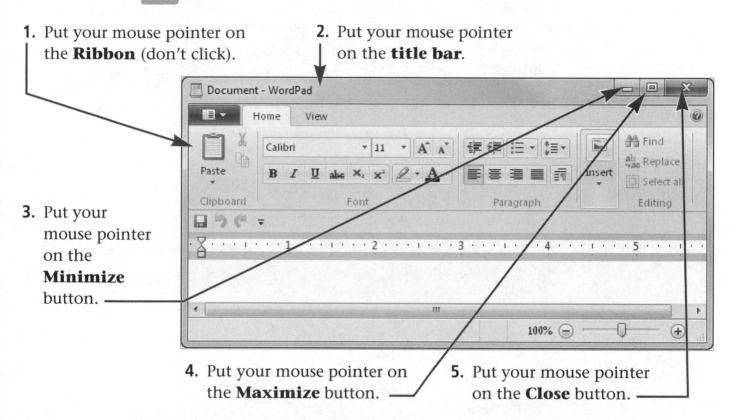

**3.** Put your mouse pointer on the **Minimize** button.

**4.** Put your mouse pointer on the **Maximize** button.

**5.** Put your mouse pointer on the **Close** button.

**6.** Make the WordPad window disappear by clicking the **Minimize** button. Look at the bottom of the screen. You will see a WordPad button on the taskbar. You did not close WordPad, you just hid the window.

**7.** Click the **WordPad** button on the taskbar to make that window show again.

**8.** Click the **Maximize** button to make WordPad fill the whole screen.

**9.** Click the **Restore** button to make WordPad smaller.

**10.** Click the **Close** button to close WordPad.

## CONCEPT 2.4  Moving a Window

Sometimes you will want to move a window to see all of it better or to see something behind it.

---

**HOW TO MOVE A WINDOW**

**A.** If the window is already maximized, click the Restore 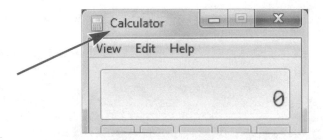 button. You cannot move a window if it is maximized to fill the whole screen.

**B.** To move a window, you must put your mouse pointer on the title bar of the window.

**C.** Hold down the left mouse button and move the mouse. You can move the window in any direction.

---

## EXERCISE 2.4  Open the Calculator Program

In this exercise, you will open the Calculator program and move the Calculator program window.

1. Open the Calculator program: **Start→All Programs→Accessories→ Calculator.**

### Move the Calculator Window

2. Put your mouse pointer on the **title bar**.

4. Release the mouse button.

3. Hold down the left mouse button and move the calculator window up.

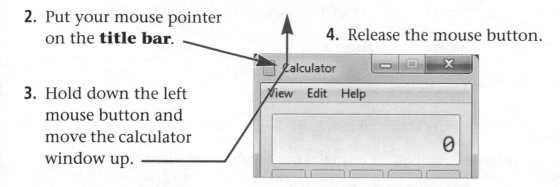

5. Hold down the mouse button while it is on the **title bar**, and keep it held down as you drag to the left. Then let go of the mouse button.

7. Hold down the mouse button and drag down. Let go of the mouse button.

6. Hold down the mouse button and drag to the right. Then let go of the mouse button.

8. Close the Calculator using the **Close** ▰ button.

# Skill Builder Exercises

SKILL BUILDER 2.1    ## Open and Move the WordPad Window

In this exercise, you will open the WordPad program. You will use the window-sizing buttons and move the WordPad window around the screen.

1. Open WordPad: **Start→All Programs→Accessories→WordPad**.

2. Find the **title bar** and the **Ribbon**.

3. If the window is not filling the screen already, click the **Maximize** 🔲 button.
   Notice that the Maximize button turns into the Restore button.

4. Click the **Restore** 🗗 button to make the window smaller again.

5. Click the **Minimize** ⎯ button.

6. Click the **WordPad** 🄰 button on the taskbar to restore the window.

7. Put your mouse pointer on the title bar and move the WordPad window to different places on the Desktop.

8. Click the **Close** ✕ button to close WordPad.

## SKILL BUILDER 2.2  Open and Move the Calculator Window

In this exercise, you will open the Calculator program and move the window around the screen.

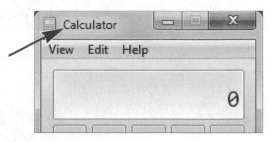

1. Open Calculator: **Start→All Programs→Accessories→Calculator**.

2. Put your mouse pointer on the **title bar**.

3. Hold down the mouse button and move the calculator to the **top-right corner** of the Desktop. Release the mouse button.

4. Move the calculator to the **bottom-right corner** of the Desktop.

5. Move the calculator to the **top-left corner** of the Desktop.

6. Move the calculator to the **bottom-left corner** of the Desktop.

7. Move the calculator to the **center** of the Desktop.

8. **Close** [ X ] the Calculator program.

## SKILL BUILDER 2.3  Personal Project: Make a List

In this exercise, you will make a list of different ways people use computers.

1. On a piece of paper, write a list of six ways people use computers at home and at work.

2. Show your list to other students in your class. Compare their lists with yours. Add at least three more computer uses to your list from other students.

 # Conversation

## Paired Conversation

With a partner, take turns reading the A and B parts of the conversation.

| | |
|---|---|
| Student A | Good morning. |
| Student B | Hi. What are we studying today? |
| Student A | I think we are going to learn how to open and close a window. |
| Student B | Do our computers have windows? |
| Student A | Yes, they can show different programs or a message. |
| Student B | Do they appear on the screen? |
| Student A | Yes. There are many windows inside your computer. |
| Student B | Oh! How do you open a window? |
| Student A | Well, we will learn that today. |
| Student B | Will we have to use the Start button? |
| Student A | Yes, and the Start menu too. |
| Student B | What are the names of some of the programs that you can see in Windows? |
| Student A | WordPad, Calculator, and Internet Explorer. |
| Student B | I know about the title bar and how to use the Minimize, Maximize, and Restore buttons. |
| Student A | That's great. You'll learn about the menu bar and the Ribbon, too. |
| Student B | What else is important to learn? |
| Student A | Well, you should know how to move a window around on the screen. |
| Student B | I can't wait to start! |

# Using Windows Programs

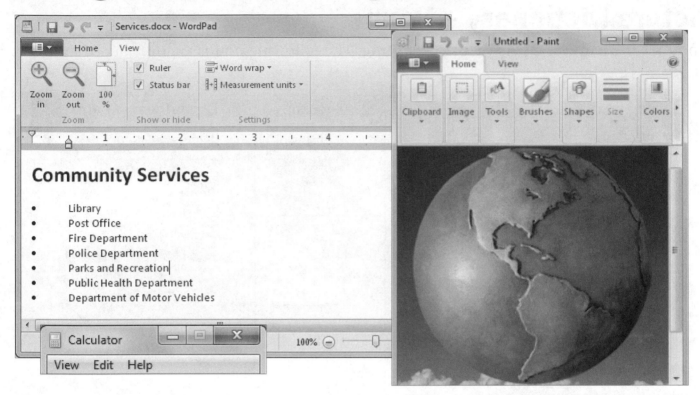

## LEARNING OBJECTIVES

After studying this lesson, you will be able to:

### Computer Objectives

- Use a program menu

- Use a program Ribbon

- Open a dialog box and work with a drop-down list

- Draw a picture in the Paint program

- Use the Calculator program

- Play a computer game

### Language Objectives

- Use vocabulary words to describe parts of different programs

- Use computer verbs to describe actions you can do with different programs

- Talk with a partner about drawing a picture in the Paint program

- Talk with a partner about the different kinds of things you can do with programs

*Student Resources labyrinthelab.com/esl3*

# Vocabulary

## Picture Dictionary – Nouns

A noun is the name of a person, place, or thing. The following nouns are introduced in this lesson:

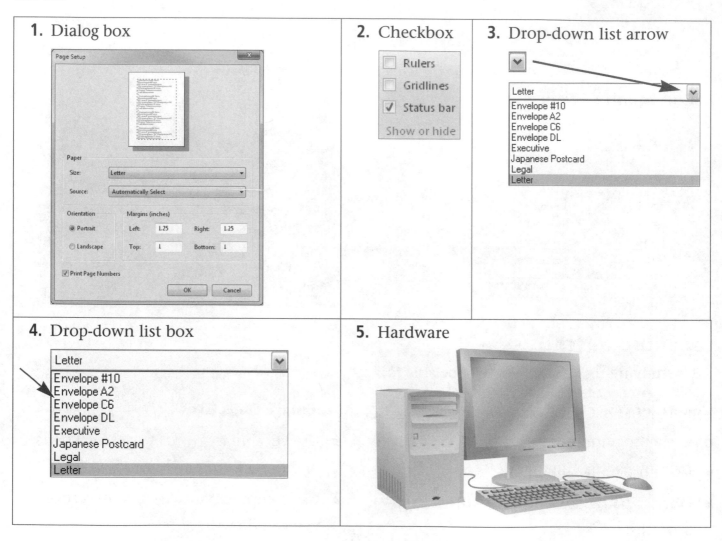

1. Dialog box

2. Checkbox

3. Drop-down list arrow

4. Drop-down list box

5. Hardware

1. **Dialog box** – A window with boxes you can click to select what you want

2. **Checkbox** – A box that you can click to select something you want

3. **Drop-down list arrow** – An arrow you can click to make the drop-down list box appear

4. **Drop-down list box** – A list with more things you can choose from

5. **Hardware** – The physical part of the computer system, such as the monitor or the keyboard

# Picture Dictionary – Nouns (continued)

**6.** Software

**7.** Appearance

**8.** Settings

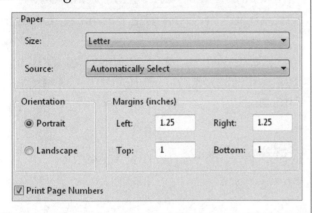

**9.** Program menu button

---

**6. Software** – Programs added to the computer system that are not hardware, such as WordPad

**7. Appearance** – The way something looks

 **NOTE!** The word "appearance" is a noun.
The word "appear" is a verb.

**8. Settings** – Information about how a program is set up

**9. Program menu button** – Button you click in WordPad and Paint to show new choices

# Computer Verbs

A verb tells an action or what a subject is or does. The following verbs are introduced in this lesson:

| VERB | MEANING | EXAMPLE |
|------|---------|---------|
| 1. Appear | When something shows and you can see it | When you click the box, a checkmark will appear inside the box. |
| 2. Check | To click a box so that a checkmark appears | When you have a few choices, you must check the one that you want. |
| 3. Clear (a box) | To click a button or box to remove what you checked before; to uncheck a box | I changed my mind, so I have to clear the box that I checked before. |
| 4. Release (a button) | To take your finger off the mouse button | After you finish your mouse action, you should release the mouse button. |
| 5. Let up | To release or let go of the button | Another way to say "release the mouse button" is to say "let up on the mouse button." |

⚠️ **NOTE!** "Release" and "Let up" are synonyms. Synonyms are words that have the same or similar meaning.

| | | |
|------|---------|---------|
| 6. Play | To use a computer game | I like to play Solitaire and other card games on my computer. |
| 7. Preview | To see how information will look when it is printed so you can decide what you want to do | I want to preview how the document will look before I print it. |
| 8. Hold (a button) | To keep your finger pressed on the mouse button | Sometimes you have to hold down your mouse button for a few seconds, and sometimes you only have to tap it. |
| 9. View | To look at something | It is important to view the tools on the toolbar so you can see the options. |

# Concepts and Exercises

CONCEPT 3.1  **Common Features in Programs**

A *program* is a set of directions that tells the computer exactly what to do to get a special kind of job done. Not all programs look the same.

Here are examples of kinds of programs that do different jobs:

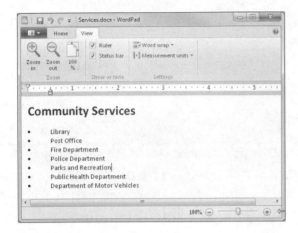

A *word-processing program* is used to type text.

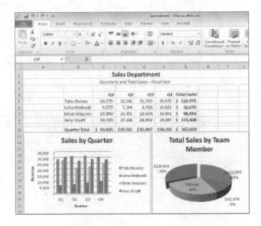

A *spreadsheet program* is used mostly for numbers.

A *graphics program* is used to make and change pictures.

A *web browser* is used to find things on the Internet.

A *computer game* is used to relax and have fun.

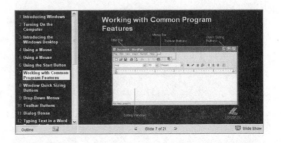

A *tutorial* is used to show and teach ideas.

Different programs have many parts that are the same. Most program windows have the following parts:

**A. Title bar** – Tells you what program you are using

**B. Ribbon** – A bar showing different icons; each icon does a different job when you click on it

**C. Buttons** – Icons that do different things when you click them with the mouse

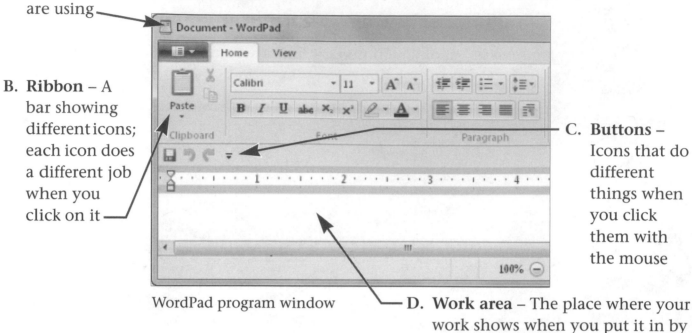

WordPad program window

**D. Work area** – The place where your work shows when you put it in by typing or using the mouse

A second example of a program is Paint.

**A. Title bar** – Tells you what program you are using

**B. Ribbon** – A bar showing different icons separated into groups; each icon does a different job when you click on it

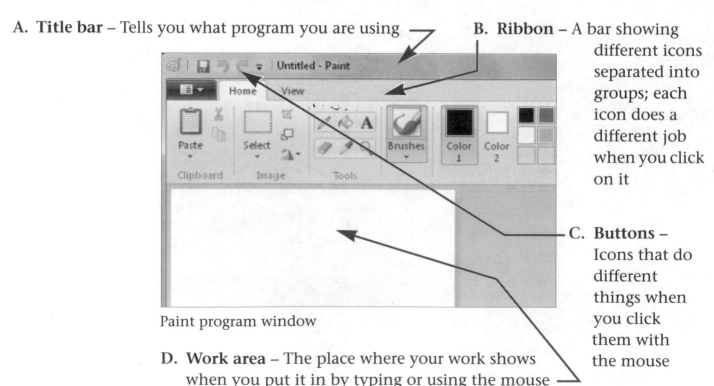

Paint program window

**C. Buttons** – Icons that do different things when you click them with the mouse

**D. Work area** – The place where your work shows when you put it in by typing or using the mouse

EXERCISE 3.1  **Open the WordPad Program**

In this exercise, you will use the Start button to start the WordPad program. Every computer with Windows has this program.

1. Open WordPad: **Start→All Programs→Accessories→WordPad**.

2. Click the **Maximize** button to make the WordPad window fill the screen.

3. Find the **title bar** on the screen and point at it with the mouse.

4. Find the **Ribbon** and the **work area**. Move your mouse pointer over each part.

5. Leave WordPad open for the next exercise.

CONCEPT 3.2 **Dialog Boxes**

Most programs have some type of dialog box. You can change settings by changing the information in a dialog box. Many dialog boxes have the following features:

**A. Checkboxes** – Click in the boxes to check or uncheck them.

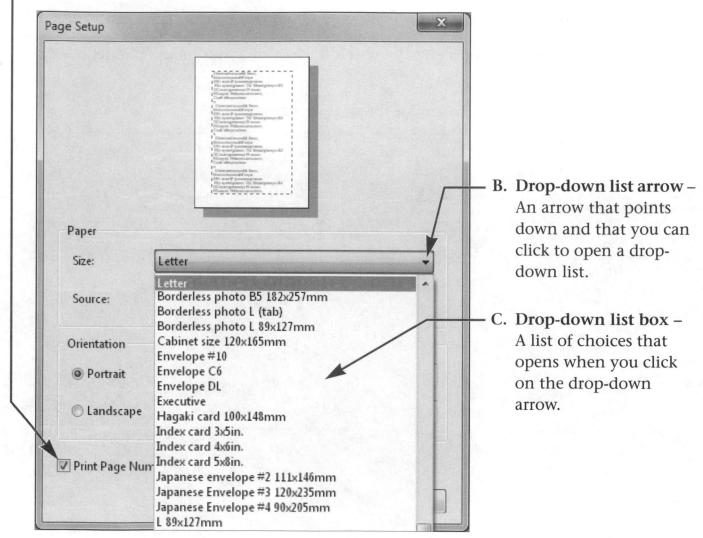

**B. Drop-down list arrow** – An arrow that points down and that you can click to open a drop-down list.

**C. Drop-down list box** – A list of choices that opens when you click on the drop-down arrow.

WordPad program dialog box

## EXERCISE 3.2  Open a Dialog Box

In this exercise, you will use a dialog box in WordPad. The program should be open from the last exercise.

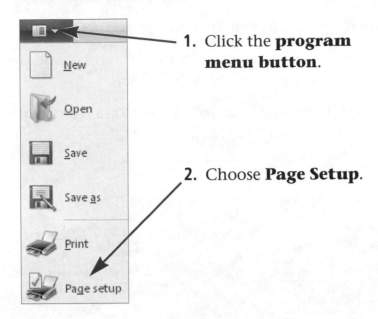

**1.** Click the **program menu button**.

**2.** Choose **Page Setup**.

The following dialog box will appear on your screen.

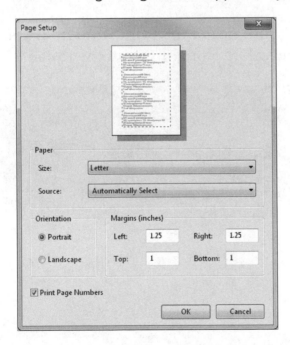

**3.** Find a **drop-down arrow**, a **drop-down list box**, and a **checkbox**.

**4.** Close the dialog box with the **Close** **X** button. Then, **close WordPad**.

## CONCEPT 3.3 **Using Tools on a Ribbon in Paint**

Paint gives you many tools to work with to make pictures. Some are easy to use and some take a while to learn. We will look at the easy ones now.

- You can use tools on a Ribbon by clicking on them.

- In Paint, when you click on a tool, a special symbol appears in place of the mouse pointer. Each tool has its own symbol.

We will not use all the tools, but only a few to see how they work. Here are some of the tools. To use a tool, click it.

**A.** Eraser

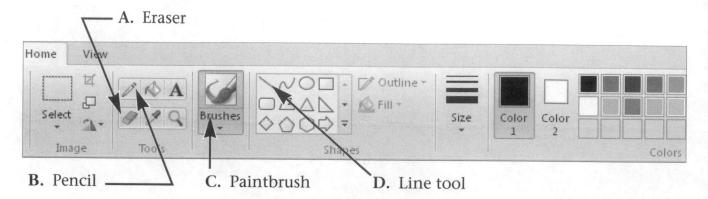

**B.** Pencil          **C.** Paintbrush          **D.** Line tool

Tools only work in the white area of the Paint window. If you want to pick a color, click on one of the colors on right side of the Home tab of the Ribbon.

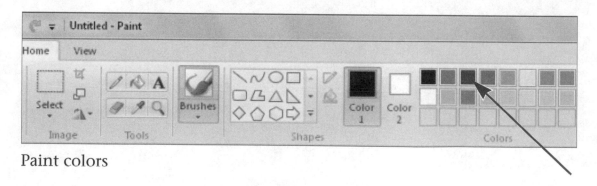

Paint colors

# Dragging

To use a tool, you need to drag with the mouse. (For a definition of "drag," see Lesson 1, Learning About Computer Basics.) Here is how:

1. Point where you want to start and then hold down your left mouse button.

2. Move the mouse to make your design.

3. Let go of the left mouse button when you are finished making the design.

You will learn how to drag in the next exercise.

EXERCISE 3.3 **Use Tools in Paint**

In this exercise, you will use some of the drawing tools in Paint. The program should still be open from the last exercise.

### Draw a Line

1. Open Paint: **Start→All Programs→Accessories→Paint**.

2. **Maximize** ☐ the Paint window.

3. Click the **Line** ◣ button on the Ribbon.

4. Point to a place on the left side of the white area. Hold down your **left mouse button**, and keep it held down until step 6.

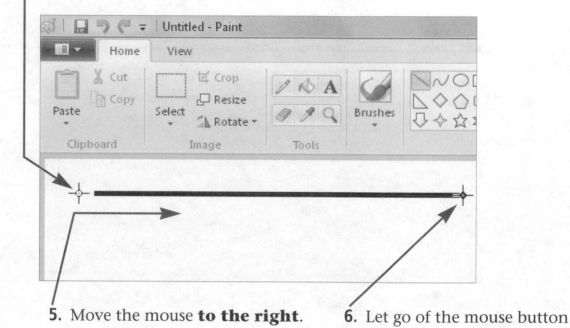

5. Move the mouse **to the right**. This draws a line.

6. Let go of the mouse button where you want to stop the line.

You should see a line.

## Draw a Box

**7.** Click the **Rectangle** tool.

**8.** Point to a place anywhere on the white area. Hold down the mouse button and move it in the direction shown while keeping the button held down.

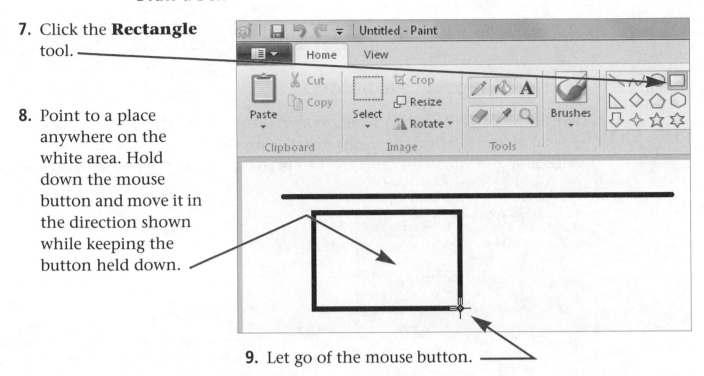

**9.** Let go of the mouse button.

## Draw a Colored Line

**10.** Click the **Pencil** tool.

**11.** Click the color **red** from the Colors box.

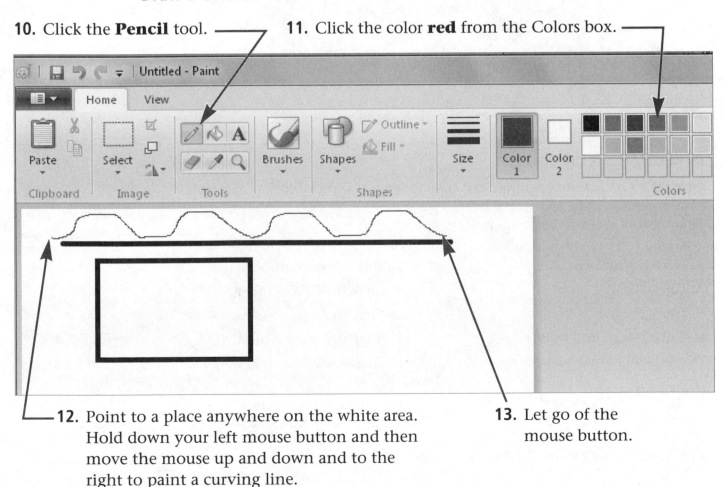

**12.** Point to a place anywhere on the white area. Hold down your left mouse button and then move the mouse up and down and to the right to paint a curving line.

**13.** Let go of the mouse button.

**14.** You can keep drawing to add anything else you like to your picture.

**15.** When you are finished, **close Paint**.

---

CONCEPT 3.4 **The Windows Calculator**

The Calculator is another useful program on the computer. You can use it to do many calculations. The program looks just like a regular handheld calculator and works the same way. You can type numbers, or you can click the number buttons.

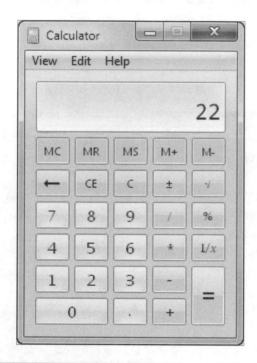

---

**HOW TO USE THE CALCULATOR**

Open the Calculator program: Start→All Programs→Accessories→Calculator.

Examples of the four basic operations:

**Add Two Numbers**

A. Click the first number.

B. Click the plus + sign.

C. Click the second number.

D. Then click the equal = sign.

**Subtract Two Numbers**

A. Click the first number.

B. Click the minus – sign.

C. Click the second number.

D. Then click the equal = sign.

**Multiply Two Numbers**
Use the * button: (3 * 2 = 6).

**Divide Two Numbers**
Use the / button: (8 / 2 = 4).

To clear a number from the Calculator, click the C (Clear) key.

## EXERCISE 3.4 Use the Calculator

In this exercise, you will use the Calculator to add and subtract. You do not have to type in the numbers. Just click the number buttons with your mouse.

1. Open Calculator: **Start→All Programs→Accessories→Calculator**.

**Add Two Numbers**

2. Click the **2 button** two times for 22.

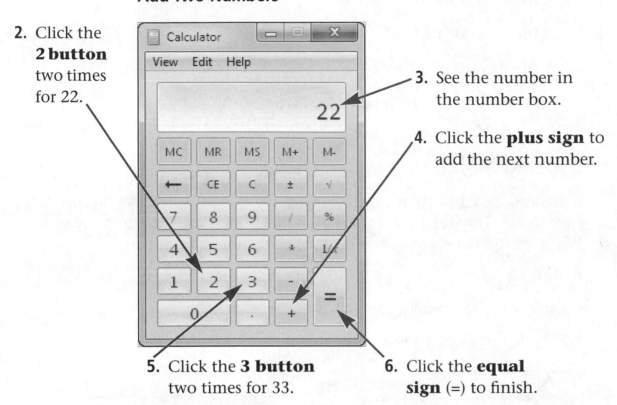

3. See the number in the number box.

4. Click the **plus sign** to add the next number.

5. Click the **3 button** two times for 33.

6. Click the **equal sign** (=) to finish.

You can see the answer (55) in the number box.

7. Click the **C button** to clear the Calculator.

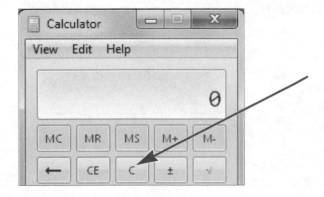

## Do Other Calculations

⚠ **IMPORTANT!** Press C to clear after you complete each of the calculations in steps 8–11.

8. Click these buttons on the calculator: **12 + 6 =**

9. Click these buttons: **100 + 75 =**

10. Click these buttons: **50 – 10 =**

11. Click these buttons: **389 – 14 =**

12. When you are finished, **close Calculator**.

---

CONCEPT 3.5  **Using a Menu**

Once you have had some practice using menus, you will find that they are easy to use. The way they work is the same from one program to the next. What changes in each program is the list of choices in the menu.

- You can open a menu by clicking on one of the words.

- Each word has its own menu that opens separately.

- When you click on some of the menu items, a dialog box will open.

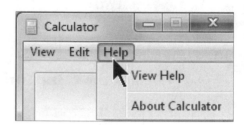

The Calculator's Help menu opens when you click Help on the menu bar.

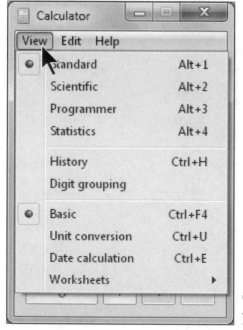

Calculator's View menu opens when you click View on the menu bar.

EXERCISE 3.5 **Use a Menu**

In this exercise, you will use a menu. Many settings can only be changed by using menus.

1. Click **View** on the menu bar. Keep your mouse over the View menu item.

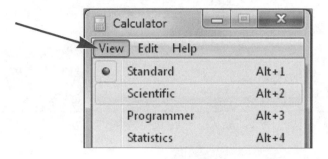

2. Click **Scientific**.

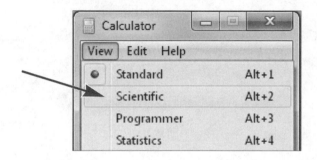

The Calculator now shows the Scientific view with more advanced buttons.

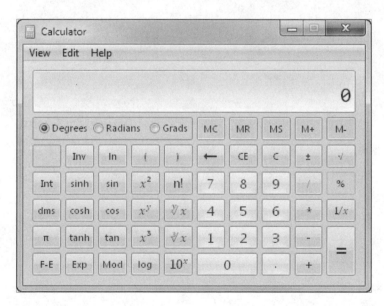

**3.** Click **View**, and then click **Standard** to return the Calculator to normal.

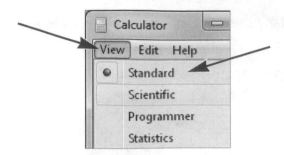

**4. Close** [ X ] the Calculator.

---

# Skill Builder Exercises

**SKILL BUILDER 3.1**    **Use Paint**

In earlier exercises, you tried some Paint tools. In this exercise, you will create a real drawing.

1. Open Paint: **Start→All Programs→Accessories→Paint**.

2. **Maximize** ▣ the Paint window.

3. Use some of the tools and colors to draw a picture of a house.

   The house doesn't have to look perfect. This is just to practice using the mouse and dragging to draw. Many programs let you do this.

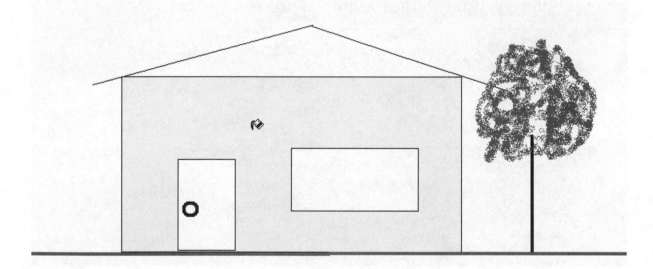

4. When you are finished, **Close** X Paint.

5. If Paint asks you if you want to save your work, click **No**.

   If you already know how to save a file, click Yes and give the file a name.

   ⚠ **NOTE!**  You will learn how to save your files in Lesson 5, Doing More with WordPad.

**Use the Calculator**

In this exercise, you will use the Calculator program to multiply, divide, and subtract numbers.

1. Open Calculator: **Start→All Programs→Accessories→Calculator**.

2. To multiply, press these buttons: **3 x 12 =**

3. To multiply, press these buttons: **25 x 2 =**

4. To divide, press these buttons: **80 / 4 =**

5. To divide, press these buttons: **36 / 12 =**

6. To subtract, press these buttons: **99 – 43 =**

7. To subtract, press these buttons: **52 – 12 =**

8. When you are finished, **close Calculator**.

**Play a Game**

In this exercise, you will learn to play Solitaire. If you have never played Solitaire with cards, ask a friend or your teacher to explain how to play the game. Playing this game will give you good practice using the mouse.

1. Open Solitaire: **Start→All Programs→Games→Solitaire**.

2. To move one of the cards, click on it. Hold down the mouse button and drag it to a new place. If you put a card in the wrong place, it will not stay there. It will jump back to where it was.

3. When you want to turn over a new card, click on the pack at the top.

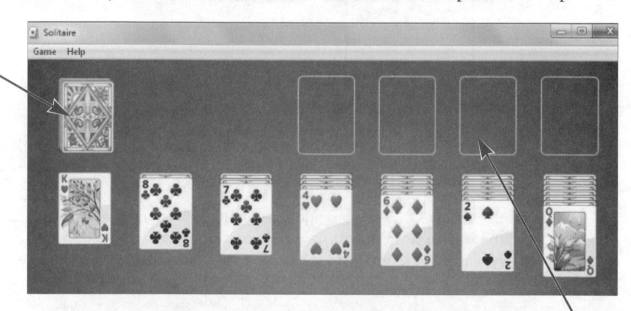

4. Start putting the aces in the four shaded areas, and build up from there. The suits (pictures on the cards) must match in each top pile. You must put all the cards in the top piles in order to win.

5. If you want to start a new game, click **Game→New Game**.

6. When you are finished playing, click the **Close**  X  button.

**Personal Project: Draw a Map**

In this exercise, you will draw and print a simple map with the Paint program.

1. Open Paint: **Start→All Programs→Accessories→Paint**.

2. Draw lines to create a simple street map of the area around your house.

    **TIP!** To draw straight lines, hold down the $\boxed{\text{Shift}}$ key as you drag a new line.

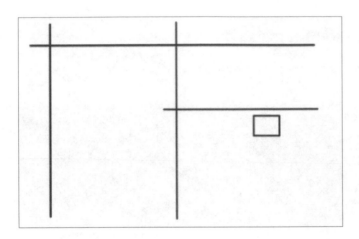

3. Use the **Text** $\boxed{A}$ tool to add street names. Click near where you want to type the words. Hold down the mouse button and drag a text box. Then you can type a street name inside the box. Make a new box for each name.

4. To print the map, click the **program menu button** ⬛▾, click **Print**, and then click **Print** again.

5. **Close Paint** without saving the map. (Or, if you know how to save a file, use **File→Save As** to save it.)

# Conversation

## Paired Conversation

With a partner, take turns reading the A and B parts of the conversation.

| | |
|---|---|
| Student A | Yesterday we learned how to minimize a window. |
| Student B | Yes, I remember. The window disappeared but did not really close. |
| Student A | Do you remember how to maximize a window? |
| Student B | Yes. Now let's talk about what we learned today. |
| Student A | Today we learned about hardware. |
| Student B | Is that like the computer and the monitor? |
| Student A | Right. We also learned about software. |
| Student B | That's like WordPad and Paint that are added into the computer. |
| Student A | That's true. |
| Student B | We also learned about the dialog boxes. |
| Student A | Yes. Dialog boxes are important because they let you select the settings that you want. |
| Student B | Did you play a computer game today? |
| Student A | Not really. I just watched somebody else play. |
| Student B | We did practice using the Paint program. |
| Student A | I liked drawing a map and typing the names of the streets. |
| Student B | Well, I'm so glad we are learning so much! |

# Creating a Document in WordPad

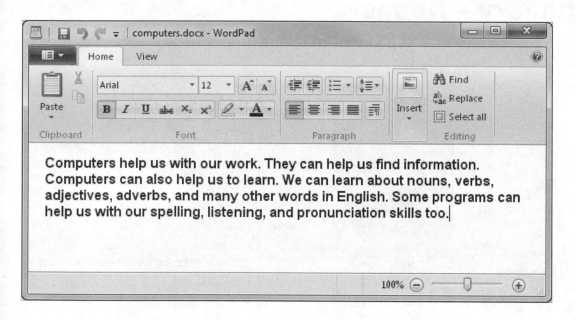

## LEARNING OBJECTIVES

After studying this lesson, you will be able to:

**Computer Objectives**

- Use the computer keyboard
- Use WordPad
- Create and edit a document
- Print a document

**Language Objectives**

- Use vocabulary words to discuss using WordPad and the keyboard
- Use computer verbs to describe how to use WordPad and the keyboard
- Use computer language to talk about how to create a document

*Student Resources* **labyrinthelab.com/esl3**

 # Vocabulary

## Picture Dictionary – Nouns

A noun is the name of a person, place, or thing. The following nouns are introduced in this lesson:

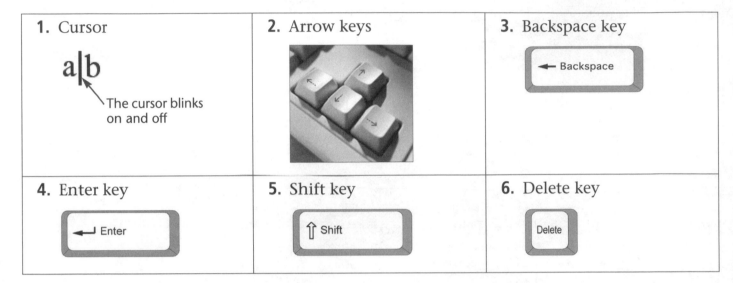

| 1. Cursor | 2. Arrow keys | 3. Backspace key |
|---|---|---|
| a\|b<br>The cursor blinks on and off | | ← Backspace |
| 4. Enter key | 5. Shift key | 6. Delete key |
| ← Enter | ⇧ Shift | Delete |

1. **Cursor** – An object on the screen that shows where you are going to type text

2. **Arrow keys** – Keys that move your cursor to another place without erasing

3. **Backspace key** – A key that erases what is to the left of the cursor

4. **Enter key** – A key that moves the cursor to the next line

5. **Shift key** – A key that helps make a capital letter or the top symbol of the typed key

 **!TIP!** Capital letters are used at the beginning of a sentence and for the first letter of names. In English, we also capitalize the first letter of the days of the week and the months of the year.

6. **Delete key** – A key that erases what is to the right of the cursor

# Picture Dictionary – Nouns (continued)

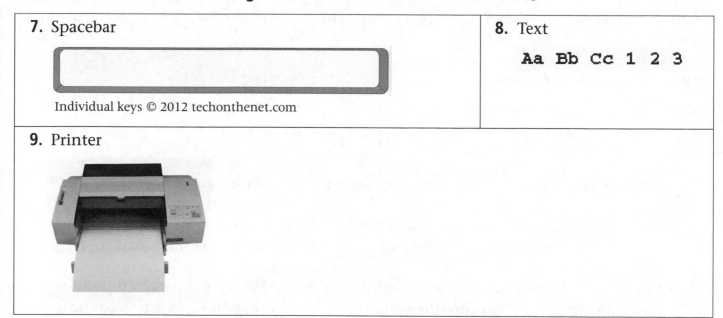

**7.** Spacebar

Individual keys © 2012 techonthenet.com

**8.** Text

Aa Bb Cc 1 2 3

**9.** Printer

**7. Spacebar** – The bar that puts a space between words

**8. Text** – The letters, numbers, and symbols you type on the keyboard

**9. Printer** – A machine that puts information from the computer onto a sheet of paper

# Computer Verbs

A verb tells an action or what a subject is or does. The following verbs are introduced in this lesson:

| VERB | MEANING | EXAMPLE |
|---|---|---|
| 1. Delete | To take away or erase | I typed the wrong word. I will delete it and type the correct word. |

> **!NOTE!** The words "erase" and "remove" are synonyms of the word "delete."

| VERB | MEANING | EXAMPLE |
|---|---|---|
| 2. Type | To use the keyboard to put information on the page | I don't know how to type, so I have to take a keyboarding class. |
| 3. Wrap | To make words automatically continue onto the next line | When you type a paragraph, the computer will wrap the words onto the next line. |
| 4. Insert (text) | To type text between two other letters or words | I forgot to type my middle name. I need to insert it between my first name and last name. |
| 5. Print | To put a document from your computer onto a sheet of paper | I finished my letter. Now I will print it and mail it to my grandmother. |

# Concepts and Exercises

**The Computer Keyboard**

The computer keyboard has more keys than a typewriter. In this lesson, you will be using only the common keys. Here are some important keyboard keys.

**A.** Shift keys          **B.** Enter key          **C.** Backspace key

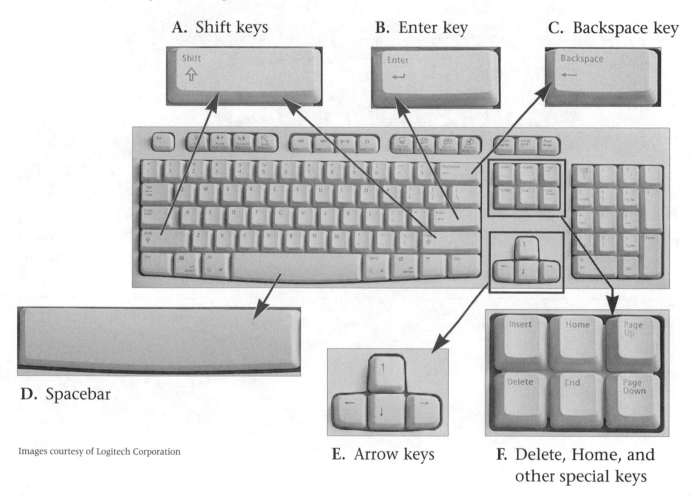

**D.** Spacebar

Images courtesy of Logitech Corporation

**E.** Arrow keys          **F.** Delete, Home, and other special keys

**EXERCISE 4.1** **Examine the Computer Keyboard**

In this exercise, you will find the keys on the computer keyboard.

**!NOTE!** Your keyboard may not look exactly like the one on this page.

**1.** Look at the computer keyboard.

**2.** Look at the **top row of keys**. None of them are on a typewriter.

**3.** Find the [Backspace] key.

**4.** Find the [Delete] key.

**5.** Find a [Shift] key.

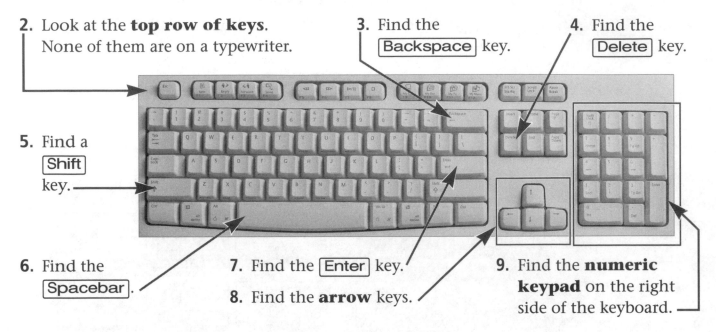

**6.** Find the [Spacebar].

**7.** Find the [Enter] key.

**8.** Find the **arrow** keys.

**9.** Find the **numeric keypad** on the right side of the keyboard.

## CONCEPT 4.2 **Using the Keyboard**

It is important to learn how to type well on a keyboard. The best way is to take a keyboarding class. Your hands should rest on the keyboard like this.

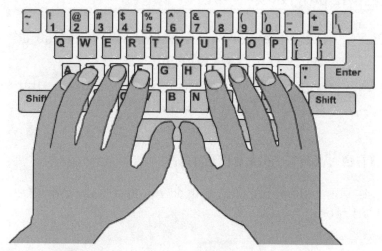

Image courtesy of learn-everything.com

 EXERCISE 4.2 **Get Ready to Type**

In this exercise, you will place your hands on the keyboard.

1. Put your hands on the keyboard with your fingers on the keys as shown above. You should feel a small bump on both the F and J keys.

2. Move your fingers up or down to touch the other keys.

## CONCEPT 4.3 Word-Processing Programs

A word-processing program helps you type on the computer. You can create letters, notes, lists, and many other things. There are two commonly used word-processing programs.

WordPad    A simple word-processing program that comes with every Windows computer

Word    A powerful word-processing program that you must buy separately and install on a computer

## EXERCISE 4.3 Start the WordPad Program

In this exercise, you will use the Start button menu to start WordPad. Then you will look at the WordPad program window.

1. Click **Start**.

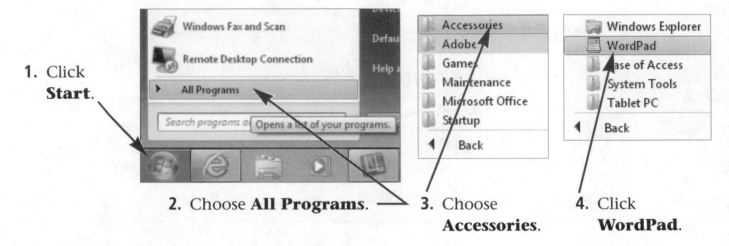

2. Choose **All Programs**.    3. Choose **Accessories**.    4. Click **WordPad**.

WordPad opens on the screen.

5. Find the **title bar** and the **Ribbon**.

Leave WordPad open.

**Typing on the Computer**

You type on the computer with the keyboard. Everything you type appears at the cursor position.

### The Cursor

The cursor is a blinking line that shows where the computer will type next. You can move the cursor anywhere you have typed. You will learn how to move it soon.

### Word Wrap

When you are typing and reach the end of a line, the computer will automatically put the next words you type on the next line for you. That is called word wrap.

- Example with Word Wrap

> Computers can help us with our work. They can help us find information. Computers can also help us to learn. We can learn about nouns, verbs, adjectives, adverbs, and many other words in English. Some programs can help us with our spelling, listening, and pronunciation skills too.

- Example without Word Wrap

> Computers can help us with our work. They can help us find information. Computers can also

### Enter Key

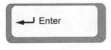

The Enter key starts a new line wherever the cursor is. You only need to use the Enter key at the end of a short line or a paragraph.

### Spacebar

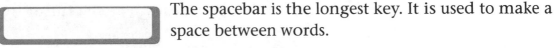

The spacebar is the longest key. It is used to make a space between words.

## EXERCISE 4.4 Type with WordPad

In this exercise, you will type in WordPad and see how word wrap works.

1. **Type the sentences** in the following paragraph.

   Do *not* press [Enter]. When there is not enough space on the line, the words will go to the next line.

   **!TIP!** Hold down the [Shift] key to make capital letters.

   ```
   Computers help us with our work. They can help us find
   information. Computers can also help us to learn. We can
   learn about nouns, verbs, adjectives, adverbs, and many
   other words in English. Some programs can help us with our
   spelling, listening, and pronunciation skills too.
   ```

   This is how your screen should look when you are finished.

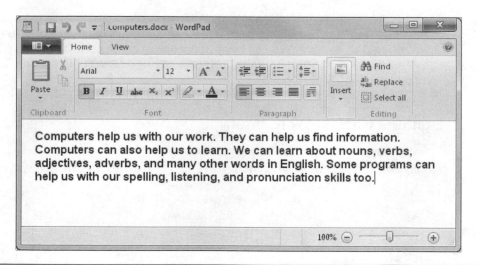

## CONCEPT 4.5 Inserting Text

You can insert text by moving the cursor and then typing. You must first put the cursor where you want using the mouse or the arrow (cursor) keys. Then when you type, the new letters appear where the cursor is blinking.

Before typing         After typing

### Arrow Keys

The arrow keys on the keyboard are also called the cursor keys. Each time you tap an arrow key, the cursor moves once in that direction.

**EXERCISE 4.5**  **Insert Text**

In this exercise, you will insert a word and insert new lines into your WordPad document.

1. Click to the left of the word "help." ─────────

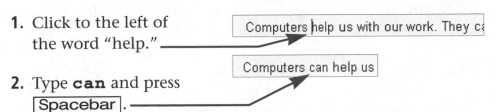

2. Type **can** and press Spacebar . ─────────

Now you will make two blank lines.

3. Move your mouse to the left of the "C" in "Computers." Click only when you see the mouse pointer change to a ⏉.

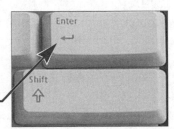

4. Press the Enter key, then press Enter again to make two new lines. ─────

5. Press the **up arrow** key two times (to get to the top of the document).

Now you are ready to type a new line.

6. Type the new line **Typing in a Word Processor** here.

Typing in a Word Processor

Computers can help us with our

It is easy to add new lines or words at any time.

CONCEPT 4.6 **Deleting Text**

You can delete (remove) letters, words, and even entire lines from a word-processing document. There are two main ways to do this: use the Delete key and use the Backspace key.

### Delete Key

This key deletes letters to the right (→) of the cursor. You remove one letter or space each time you tap the Delete key.

A. Cursor

B. [Delete] [Delete]
   [Delete] [Delete]

**Before Delete**
Computers | can help us with our work.

**After Delete**
Computers help us with our work.

### Backspace Key

This key deletes letters to the left (←) of the cursor. You remove one letter or space each time you tap the Backspace key.

A. Cursor

**Before Backspace**
Computers can | help us with our work.

**After Backspace Delete**
Computers help us with our work.

B. [Backspace] [Backspace]
   [Backspace] [Backspace]

**EXERCISE 4.6** **Delete Text**

In this exercise, you will delete some words from your document. Then you will close the WordPad program.

### Use the Delete Key

**1.** Click to the left of the word "can" in the second line of text.

**2.** Press Delete Delete Delete Delete so the word "can" and the space after it are erased.

Typing in a Word Processor

Computers help us with our

### Use the Backspace Key

**3.** Click to the right of the sentence "They can help us find information."

Typing in a Word Processor

Computers help us with our work. They can help us find information. Computers

**4.** Press Backspace until the whole sentence is gone and one more time to take out the extra space.

This is what the screen should look like after step 4.

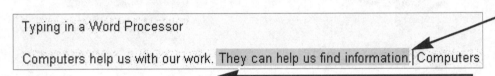

Typing in a Word Processor

Computers help us with our work. Computers can also help us to learn

## CONCEPT 4.7 **Printing Your Work**

You will often want to print documents that you type. Some programs have two methods you can use to give the print command.

To print, click program menu button 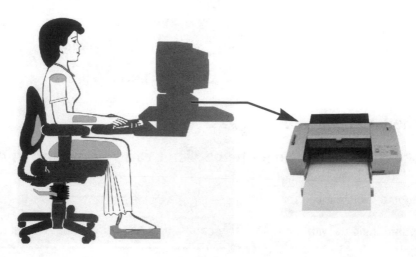 →Print→ Print . Your computer sends the document to the printer and the printer puts it onto the paper.

## EXERCISE 4.7 Print Your Document

In this exercise, you will add your name to your WordPad file, save it, and then print it.

1. Use the **arrow keys or the mouse** to go to the very bottom of your WordPad document text.

2. Press ⎡Enter⎤ two times.

3. **Type your name** at the bottom of the document.

4. Click **program menu button** 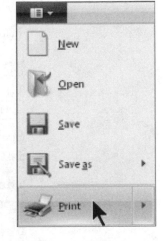 →**Print**.

5. When the Print dialog box opens, click [ Print ] to finish the command.

6. Go to the printer and get your document.

7. **Close** [ X ] the WordPad window.

   WordPad will ask if you wish to save changes to your document.

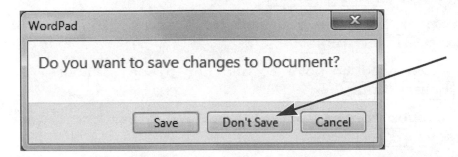

8. Click **Don't Save** to close the WordPad program without saving your document.

   You will learn how to save your documents in Lesson 5, Doing More with WordPad.

# Skill Builder Exercises

SKILL BUILDER 4.1    **Type Sentences**

In this exercise, you will type a simple document with WordPad.

1. Open WordPad: **Start→All Programs→Accessories→WordPad**.

2. Type the following sentences.

   Use Shift to make capital letters. Only press Enter where it appears below.

   **The cursor shows where you are going to type text.** Enter
   Enter

   **You use a keyboard when you want to put letters or numbers into the computer.** Enter  Enter

   **The Shift key lets you type a capital letter or the top symbol on a key.** Enter  Enter

   **Press the Enter key when you want to start typing text on another line.** Enter  Enter

   **Arrow keys are used to move to another place without erasing.** Enter  Enter

   **Place the cursor to the left of text and press the Delete key to erase.** Enter  Enter

   **Place the cursor to the right of text and press the Backspace key to erase.** Enter

3. Click **program menu button** ▤▾ →**Print**→ [ Print ] to print your work.

4. **Close** [ X ] WordPad. Click **Don't Save** when WordPad asks if you want to save your work.

**Type the Punctuation Marks**

In this exercise, you will type a list of punctuation marks with WordPad. Then you will insert a title for the list.

1. Open WordPad: **Start→All Programs→Accessories→WordPad**.

2. Type the following sentences.

   You must use [Shift] to type some of the punctuation marks. Only press [Enter] where it appears below.

. **A period is used at the end of a statement or a command.** [Enter]

, **A comma is used to separate words or phrases.** [Enter]

: **A colon is used to introduce a list.** [Enter]

! **An exclamation mark is used at the end of a sentence that shows surprise or strong feeling.** [Enter]

? **A question mark is used at the end of every sentence that asks a question.** [Enter]

When you finish, your screen should look like this:

. A period is used at the end of a statement or a command.
, A comma is used to separate words or phrases.
: A colon is used to introduce a list.
! An exclamation mark is used at the end of a sentence that shows surprise or strong feeling.
? A question mark is used at the end of every sentence that asks a question.|

### Insert a Title for the List

**3.** Put the cursor at the **top left** of the list. (Use the arrow keys.)

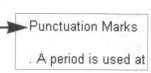

**4.** Press ⌗Enter⌗ two times.

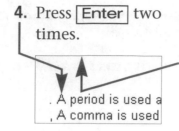

**5.** Press the **up arrow** key two times (to move the cursor to the top).

**6.** Type the title **Punctuation Marks** here.

> Punctuation Marks
>
> . A period is used at

Now your screen should look like this:

> Punctuation Marks|
>
> . A period is used at the end of a statement or a command.
> , A comma is used to separate words or phrases.
> : A colon is used to introduce a list.
> ! An exclamation mark is used at the end of a sentence that shows surprise or strong feeling.
> ? A question mark is used at the end of every sentence that asks a question.

**7.** Click **program menu button** ▤▾ →**Print**→ [ Print ] to print your work.

**8.** **Close** [ X ] WordPad.

**9.** Click **Don't Save** when WordPad asks if you wish to save your work.

**Type a Paragraph**

In this exercise, you will type a paragraph with WordPad.

1. Open WordPad: **Start→All Programs→Accessories→WordPad**.

2. Type the following paragraph.

   Do *not* press [Enter] until the end of the paragraph. Let Word Wrap move your words to the next line for you. Your lines will probably end at different places than they do in this example.

   ```
   English as a Second Language (ESL) classes teach English to
   students from other countries that are now living in the
   United States. Students can take these classes at high
   schools, adult schools, and community colleges. ESL classes
   are offered at beginning, intermediate, and advanced levels.
   [Enter]
   ```

3. Click **program menu button** [≡▼] →**Print**→ [ Print ] to print your work.

4. **Close** [ X ] WordPad.

5. Click **Don't Save** when WordPad asks if you wish to save your work.

---

**Personal Project: Type a List**

In this exercise, you will type a list of things to do. Then you will print the list.

1. Open WordPad: **Start→All Programs→Accessories→WordPad**.

2. Read the following instructions and then type your list:
   - Type a list of examples of healthy foods.
   - Be sure to start with a title.
   - Press [Enter] at the end of each one so you will have one example on each line.

3. Click **program menu button** [≡▼] →**Print**→ [ Print ] to print your work.

4. **Close** [ X ] WordPad.

5. Click **Don't Save** when WordPad asks if you wish to save your work.

---

 # Conversation

## Paired Conversation

With a partner, take turns reading the A and B parts of the conversation.

| | |
|---|---|
| Student A | Hello. Are you learning to use the computer? |
| Student B | Yes, I am. |
| Student A | Will you show me how to type a résumé so I can look for a job? |
| Student B | Yes. We will learn how to do that later. First, we need to learn to use the WordPad program. |
| Student A | I don't know how to do that. |
| Student B | To open WordPad, first click the Start button. Then click All Programs, Accessories, and WordPad. |
| Student A | Oh! I see "WordPad" on the title bar! |
| Student B | Do you see the cursor blinking on the screen? |
| Student A | Yes, I do. |
| Student B | The computer is telling you that it is ready for you to type your text. |
| Student A | Is there anything else I should know before I start? |
| Student B | Yes. At the end of a paragraph, press the Enter key. |
| Student A | Okay. Anything else? |
| Student B | You can also erase a word with the Backspace key. |
| Student A | Thanks so much for helping me. |
| Student B | You're welcome. |

# Doing More with WordPad

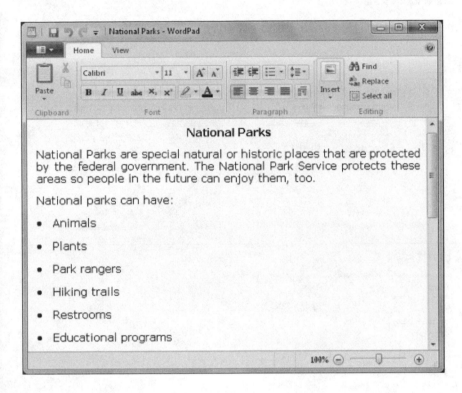

## LEARNING OBJECTIVES

After studying this lesson, you will be able to:

### Computer Objectives

- Save and name a file
- Format and align text in various ways
- Add bullets to a list

### Language Objectives

- Use appropriate words to describe saving and naming files
- Describe how to format and align text
- Tell a partner how to perform tasks learned in this lesson

*Student Resources* **labyrinthelab.com/esl3**

# Vocabulary

## Picture Dictionary – Nouns

A noun is the name of a person, place, or thing. The following nouns are introduced in this lesson:

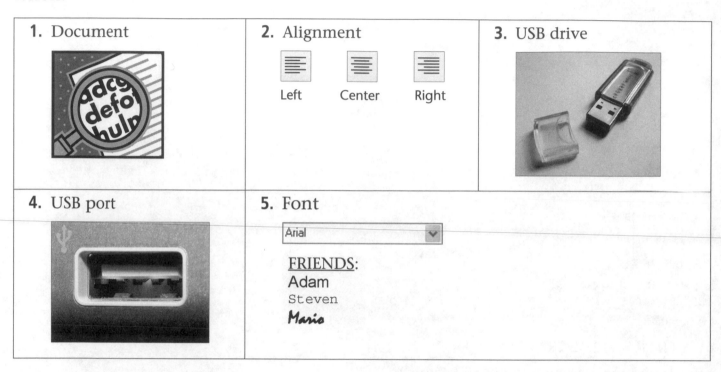

| 1. Document | 2. Alignment | 3. USB drive |
| --- | --- | --- |
| | Left  Center  Right | |

| 4. USB port | 5. Font |
| --- | --- |
| | Arial  |
| | FRIENDS:  Adam  Steven  Mario |

1. **Document** – Something that is typed and provides information

2. **Alignment** – How text is placed, either on the left, center, or right side of the page

3. **USB (Universal Serial Bus) drive** – A small tool used to save computer files; you can use it in different computers

4. **USB port** – A small opening on the CPU where you insert a USB drive

5. **Font** – The shape and size of typed letters

**!NOTE!** The word "alignment" is a synonym for the words "placement" and "location."

# Picture Dictionary – Nouns (continued)

| **6. Bullets** | **7. Bold type** | **8. Italic type** |
|---|---|---|
| ⊟ • Oranges<br>   • Apples<br>   • Bananas<br>   • Grapes | **B** **Oranges**<br>**Apples**<br>**Bananas**<br>**Grapes** | *I* *Oranges*<br>*Apples*<br>*Bananas*<br>*Grapes* |

**6. Bullets** – Special dots, squares, checkmarks, or characters that you can put before items on a list

**7. Bold type** – A style of lettering where the letters are thicker and darker

**8. Italic type** – A style of lettering where the letters are a little slanted to the right

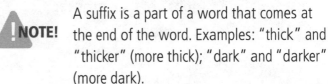 **NOTE!** A suffix is a part of a word that comes at the end of the word. Examples: "thick" and "thicker" (more thick); "dark" and "darker" (more dark).

# Computer Verbs

A verb tells an action or what a subject is or does. The following verbs are introduced in this lesson:

| VERB | MEANING | EXAMPLE |
|---|---|---|
| 1. Save | To keep what you did on a document in the computer so you can use it again later | I want to save this letter so I can remember what I wrote. |
| 2. Insert | To put a USB drive into the USB port of a computer | I have a document on this USB drive. I will insert it in the USB port so I can open the document I need. |
| 3. Increase | To make something bigger | I can't read the words. I'm going to increase the font size so the words appear larger. |
| 4. Decrease | To make something smaller | The letters are too big and the document is on two pages. Please decrease the font size so the document fits on one page. |
| 5. Align | To place on the left, center, or right side of the page | Most documents that we type are aligned on the left side of the page. |
| 6. Scroll | To move the contents of a window up, down, right, or left | When you use the Font menu, you have to scroll down to find the font you like. |
| 7. Highlight | To click at the beginning of a letter and drag the mouse to the end of what you want to change | To change the text of this sentence, you have to highlight it first. |
| 8. Format (font) | To pick the font you want and use it in your document | I don't like the font on this letter, so I am going to format it with a new font type. |
| 9. Right-click | To press and release the right mouse button | You usually left-click the mouse button, but sometimes you have to right-click it. |

# Concepts and Exercises

**CONCEPT 5.1**  ## Highlighting Text

To change the format of text, you must highlight it first. You can see that text is highlighted when the background becomes blue (or another color), as shown here.

**A.** Text not highlighted          **B.** Text highlighted

> It is fun to change the format of my text. It makes my work look better. Formatting also makes my words more interesting and easy to read. I can show which words are important.

---

**HOW TO HIGHLIGHT TEXT**

Steps A–C show one way to highlight text, by dragging with the mouse.

 **NOTE!**     You can highlight text from the beginning to the end or from the end to the beginning.

**A.** Click at the right end of the text that you want to highlight.

> It is fun to change the format of my text. It makes my work look better. Formatting also makes my words more interesting and easy to read. I can show which words are important.

**B.** Hold down the left mouse button and then move up and to the left as you continue to hold down the mouse button (dragging).

**C.** Let go of the mouse button when all of the text is selected.

**HOW TO REMOVE HIGHLIGHTING**

Click anywhere away from the highlighted words to take off the highlighting.

EXERCISE 5.1 **Highlight Text**

In this exercise, you will type text in WordPad and then drag with the mouse to highlight some of the text.

1. Open WordPad: **Start→All Programs→Accessories→WordPad**.

2. Type the following paragraph in WordPad:

   `It is fun to change the format of my text. It makes my work look better. Formatting also makes my words more interesting and easy to read. I can show which words are important.`

   Now you will highlight the first sentence.

3. Move your mouse pointer to the end of the first sentence.

   It is fun to change the format of my text. It makes my words more interesting and easy to read. I can show v

4. Hold down the mouse button and move to the left until the first sentence is highlighted.

   It is fun to change the format of my text. It makes my words more interesting and easy to read. I can show

5. Let go of the mouse button.

   The first sentence should look like this. The highlighted text is also called a selection.

   It is fun to change the format of my text. It makes my work look better. Formatting also makes my words more interesting and easy to read. I can show which words are important.

6. Click on a clear part of the WordPad window (away from the highlight) to remove the highlight.

   Leave WordPad open. You will soon learn something new to do with a selection.

**82** Lesson 5 | Doing More with WordPad

CONCEPT 5.2  **Formatting Text**

Formatting is done to make the text that you type look better. One way you can make it look different is by changing the font shape and size. Here are some examples of different font types.

| Font Name | Example |
|---|---|
| Times New Roman | This text is formatted with the Times New Roman font. |
| Arial Black | **This text is formatted with the Arial Black font.** |
| French Script | *This text is formatted with the French Script font.* |
| Papyrus | This text is formatted with the Papyrus font. |

**!NOTE!** In this lesson, the word "format" is used in the present tense, as a gerund, and in the past tense. For example, notice the spelling change in the words "format," "formatting," and "formatted."

Fonts can be different sizes.

| 10 pt. | 12 pt. | 18 pt. | 24 pt. | 36 pt. |
|---|---|---|---|---|
| ABC | ABC | ABC | ABC | ABC |

Here are some other ways to format text:

| Normal | Bold | Italics | Underline |
|---|---|---|---|
| ABC | **ABC** | *ABC* | <u>ABC</u> |

To change the format of any text, you must highlight it first.

# The WordPad Ribbon

One way to format text you have highlighted is to use the Ribbon. (If you don't see the icons on your Ribbon, double-click the Home tab.) Some features of the WordPad Ribbon are shown here.

**A. Font Type drop-down button –** Click this button to change the font type. ————

**B. Font Size drop-down button –** Click this button to change the font size.

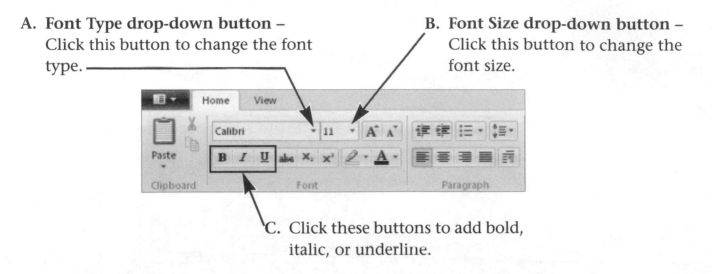

C. Click these buttons to add bold, italic, or underline.

Watch your text change as you change the font settings.

**EXERCISE 5.2** **Format Text in WordPad**

In this exercise, you will highlight text and apply a font format to it.

1. Highlight the word "fun" in the first sentence, as in the picture.

It is **fun** to change

2. Click the **Font Type drop-down button** and then click **Arial Black**. (You may have to scroll down to see it.)

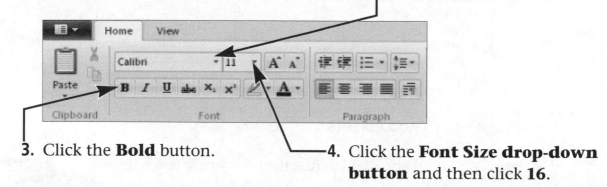

3. Click the **Bold** button.

4. Click the **Font Size drop-down button** and then click **16**.

5. Highlight the word "work" in the second sentence on the first line so you can change the font type and format of that word.

6. Click the **Font Type drop-down arrow** and then click **Courier New**. (You may need to scroll down to find it.)

7. Click the **Italic** $I$ button.

8. Click the **Font Size drop-down arrow** and then click **16**.
   See how the word "work" looks different now. Leave WordPad open.

## CONCEPT 5.3  Adding Bullets

You add bullets to make lines of text look more like a list.

Days of the Week
Sunday
Monday
Tuesday
Wednesday
Thursday
Friday
Saturday

Without bullets

Days of the Week
• Sunday
• Monday
• Tuesday
• Wednesday
• Thursday
• Friday
• Saturday

With bullets

**HOW TO ADD BULLETS**

**A.** To add bullets, highlight the lines where you want the bullets.

**B.** Then, click the Bullets button on the toolbar.

## EXERCISE 5.3  Add Bullets to a List

In this exercise, you will type a new list and apply bullets to it.

**1.** Click with your mouse at the very end of the last line of text.

**2.** Press [Enter] three times.

Now your screen should look like this.

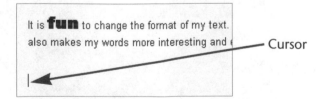

Cursor

**3.** Type the first six months of the year, as shown here. Press [Enter] after each month.

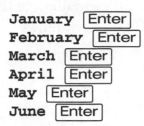

January [Enter]
February [Enter]
March [Enter]
April [Enter]
May [Enter]
June [Enter]

**4.** Highlight all of the months.

**5.** Click the **Bullets** ≔ button on the Ribbon.

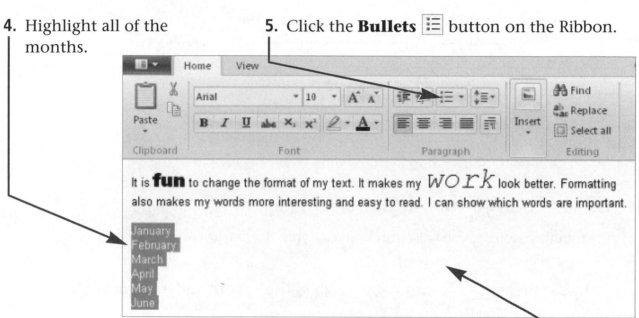

**6.** Click anywhere on a clear part of the screen to make the highlight disappear.

Now the list should look like this:

| • | January |
| • | February |
| • | March |
| • | April |
| • | May |

Leave WordPad open.

| • | June |

## CONCEPT 5.4 Changing the Alignment

You can use the buttons on the WordPad toolbar to change the alignment of a line. WordPad lets you choose three kinds of alignment.

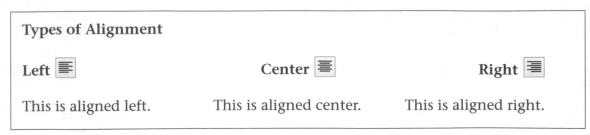

Types of Alignment

Left  Center  Right

This is aligned left.  This is aligned center.  This is aligned right.

---

**HOW TO CHANGE THE ALIGNMENT**

A. First, click somewhere in the line or paragraph you want to change.

B. Then, click the button for the kind of alignment that you want.

---

## EXERCISE 5.4 Change the Alignment

In this exercise, you will create a title for your document and change its alignment to Center.

1. Use the mouse or arrow keys to go to the very top of your document.

2. Press [Enter] two times.

3. Use the **up arrow** key to go back to the top of the document.

4. Type **Formatting Text** as the title.

Formatting Text

It is **fun** to change the

5. Click the **Center** alignment button on the Ribbon.

WordPad moves the title to the center of the screen. Leave WordPad open.

---

CONCEPT 5.5 **Saving Your Work**

In the following exercises, you will save your work to a USB drive. Your teacher will tell you if you should save it somewhere else. When you save your work on a USB drive, you can move it from one computer to another. You can also open work you did earlier and add to it or change it.

In order to save work to a USB drive, you must first insert the USB drive into the USB port on the CPU.

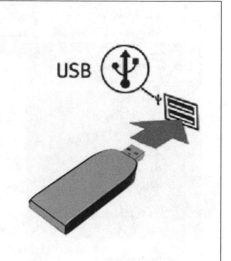

**HOW TO INSERT A USB DRIVE INTO A USB PORT**

A. Find the USB port on the CPU. It can be on the front, side, or back of the computer. Your teacher will tell you where to look on your computer.

B. Gently push the USB drive into the USB port. If it does not go into the port easily, turn it over and try it again.

C. You should be able to easily push it all the way in.

D. If any windows open automatically, close them.

## Computer Files

When you save your work on the computer, it is saved in a package called a file. Each file must be given a name so you can find it again when you need it. Once you save work to a file, you can open it again later with the same program. The process of creating a file is called saving. Your screen may look different from the picture here.

Examples of computer files

## HOW TO SAVE A FILE

**A.** Create some work in the computer program. For example, type a document in WordPad.

**B.** Click the program menu button ![menu button] →Save As.

**C.** Type the filename. You do not have to click there because it is already highlighted.

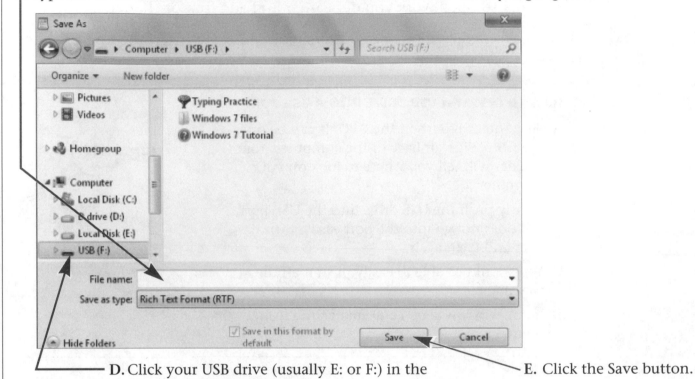

**D.** Click your USB drive (usually E: or F:) in the Navigation Pane on the left side of the dialog box.

**E.** Click the Save button.

After you finish your computer work, you must remove (take out) the USB drive properly.

## HOW TO SAFELY REMOVE A USB DRIVE

A. Click the Show Hidden Icons button on the taskbar at the bottom-right side of the screen.

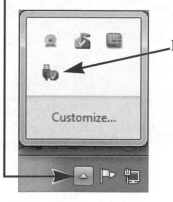

B. From the pop-up menu, click Safely Remove Hardware and Eject Media.

C. Click Eject. Each brand of USB drive has a different name. Your teacher can show you if you are not sure.

D. When the computer tells you that it is safe to remove your hardware, you can pull your USB drive out of the USB port.

## EXERCISE 5.5  Save a WordPad File

In this exercise, you will save the work that is in WordPad now. Your USB drive should be inserted into the computer. If any new windows open, close them.

1. Click **program menu button** 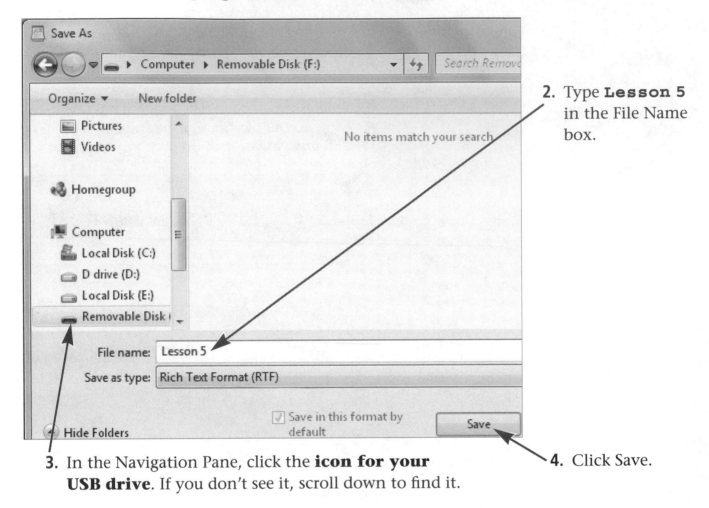 →**Save As**.

2. Type **Lesson 5** in the File Name box.

3. In the Navigation Pane, click the **icon for your USB drive**. If you don't see it, scroll down to find it.

4. Click Save.

WordPad saves your work to the computer. Leave WordPad open.

# Skill Builder Exercises

**SKILL BUILDER 5.1**  ## Change the Font

In this exercise, you will change fonts in a WordPad document.

1. Open WordPad: **Start→All Programs→Accessories→WordPad**.

2. Type this paragraph.

   Do not press Enter until the very end.

   > I am learning to do many things on my computer. I would like to practice using the computer by typing one of my favorite recipes. I like to bake carrot cake. That would be a perfect recipe for me to type in the computer. Then, I could print it and share it with my friends. I plan to learn much more!

3. Highlight the first sentence.

4. Change the font to **Wide Latin, 14, bold**.

5. Click at the end of the first sentence and press Enter.

6. Click in the middle of the first sentence and click the **Center** ☰ alignment button.

   When you are finished, you screen should look like this:

   > ### I am learning to do many things on my computer.
   >
   > I would like to practice using the computer by typing one of my favorite recipes. I like to cook carrot cake. That would be a perfect recipe for me to type in the computer. Then, I could print it and share it with my friends. I plan to learn much more!

7. **Save** the file as **Practice**. (Save it to your USB drive or wherever your teacher tells you to.)

8. Click **program menu button** ▤▾→**Print**→ Print to print your work.

9. **Close** ☒ WordPad.

**Type a Bulleted List**

In this exercise, you will type a list with bullets.

1. Open WordPad: **Start→All Programs→Accessories→WordPad**.

2. Type the following words, pressing Enter where shown.

   **Community Services** Enter
   **Library** Enter
   **Post Office** Enter
   **Fire Department** Enter
   **Police Department** Enter
   **Parks and Recreation** Enter
   **Public Health Department** Enter
   **Department of Motor Vehicles** Enter

3. Highlight the first line.

4. Change the font to **bold** and any **size and type** that you like.

5. Highlight all lines of words except the top one.

6. Click the **Bullets** button on the Ribbon.

7. **Save** the file as **Services** to your USB drive or wherever your teacher tells you to.

8. **Print** your work and then **close WordPad**.

**Change the Alignment**

In this exercise, you will change the text alignment.

1. Open WordPad: **Start→All Programs→Accessories→WordPad**.

2. Type the following words, pressing Enter where shown.

   **Central Valley School** Enter
   **1183 Riverside Drive** Enter
   **Pleasant Hill, CA 94523** Enter
   Enter
   **Dear Mr. Martinez:** Enter

3. Highlight the first line and then press the **Center** ≡ button to center it.

4. Highlight the second and third lines and then **right align** ≡ them.

5. Highlight the last line and then **left align** ≡ it.

6. **Save** the file as **Central Valley** to your USB drive or wherever your teacher tells you to.

7. **Print** your work and then **close WordPad**.

---

**Personal Project: Create a List**

In this exercise, you will create your own bulleted list.

1. Open WordPad: **Start→All Programs→Accessories→WordPad**.

2. **Type a list** of ten cities in the United States.

3. Give each city a different **font type**.

4. Highlight all of the cities.

5. Click the **Bullets** ≔ button.

6. **Save** the file as **Cities** to your USB drive or wherever your teacher tells you to.

7. **Print** your work and then **close WordPad**.

# Conversation

## Paired Conversation

With a partner, take turns reading the A and B parts of the conversation.

⚠️ **!NOTE!** This conversation uses the future tense, as seen in "going to" and "will." When you use helping verbs like these, you also need a main verb.

This conversation also uses contractions. When you put two words together, an apostrophe shows that a letter (or letters) has been left out. Here are the contractions used in this conversation:

| Contraction | Full Words |
|---|---|
| We'll | We Will |
| That's | That is |
| Don't | Do not |
| I'll | I will |
| I'm | I am |

| | |
|---|---|
| Student A | Today's lesson is going to be fun. |
| Student B | Really? Why? |
| Student A | We are going to learn how to format our text. |
| Student B | I heard someone say that we will learn about fonts. |
| Student A | Yes, we will learn how to change our text. |
| Student B | That sounds like fun! |
| Student A | I know. We'll also learn how to make bold text. |
| Student B | That's good, but I like the way italic text looks better. |
| Student A | Well, we will learn both! |
| Student B | Did you bring your USB drive? |

| | |
|---|---|
| Student A | Yes I did, but I don't know how to insert it in the computer. |
| Student B | I'll show you how to put it in the USB port. |
| Student A | Thanks. I don't want to mess it up. |
| Student B | We can put all this new formatting in our own documents. |
| Student A | Do you think we will be able to print today? |
| Student B | I think so. |
| Student A | We have a nice printer in the classroom. |
| Student B | Well, I'm going to be the first one to print my document! |

LESSON 6

# Working with Files, Folders, and Windows Help and Support

## LEARNING OBJECTIVES

After studying this lesson, you will be able to:

### Computer Objectives

- Use Windows Help and Support to answer questions
- Work with the Computer window and basic file management
- Save a file and then find and open it again later
- Use double-click to open computer files

### Language Objectives

- Use vocabulary words to describe using files and folders
- Use vocabulary words to describe parts of the Computer window, including files and folders
- Use computer verbs to describe how to find things in Windows Help and Support
- Talk with a partner about saving files
- Talk with a partner about how to play sound files on the Computer window

*Student Resources* **labyrinthelab.com/esl3**

# Vocabulary

## Picture Dictionary – Nouns

A noun is the name of a person, place, or thing. The following nouns are introduced in this lesson:

| | | |
|---|---|---|
| **1.** Folder  | **2.** Hard drive  | **3.** Computer window  |
| **4.** C: drive 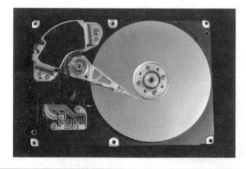 | **5.** Views button  | **6.** Address bar  |

1. **Folder** – A place where you can organize and keep computer files

2. **Hard drive** – Inside the computer, the hard drive holds all computer programs, including Windows; the information stays on the drive even after the computer is turned off

3. **Computer window** – Also called Windows Explorer; shows you the storage areas, files, and folders in your computer

4. **C: drive** – A permanent hard drive inside the computer that holds the software that makes your computer work; it can also hold your files

5. **Views button** – A button that appears in different windows that is used to change how the files look on the screen; the Views button looks different with each view that is used

6. **Address bar** – A bar near the top of the Computer window that tells you where you are looking in the computer

# Computer Verbs

A verb tells an action or what a subject is or does. The following verbs are introduced in this lesson:

| VERB | MEANING | EXAMPLE |
|------|---------|---------|
| 1. Double-click | To quickly press and release the left mouse button two times | Sometimes you need to double-click the mouse button to open a window. |
| 2. Search | A program feature that lets you look for something specific in your computer | I forgot how to make the words on my screen look larger. I have to search Windows Help and Support to find out how. |
| 3. Sort | To put things in order according to name, size, or date | I have so many files! I'm going to sort them by date so I can see which ones are the newest ones. |
| 4. Modify | To make a small change to something in order to improve it | I wrote a letter yesterday, but I need to modify it because I thought of one more sentence to write. |
| 5. Play | To listen to a music file or to watch a video file | Do you want to play the new music file that I downloaded from the Internet? |
| 6. Choose | To select (or to click on) something from a group of different things | My favorite colors are red, yellow, blue, and green. I will choose one for the font in the letter to my friend so it will be brighter. |
| 7. View | To look at something | I want to view the documents in that folder in different ways, so I will click the Views button. |

# Concepts and Exercises

CONCEPT 6.1  **The Computer Window**

In the Computer window, also called Windows Explorer, you can see the places where files can be saved. You can also open those places to see the files that are there.

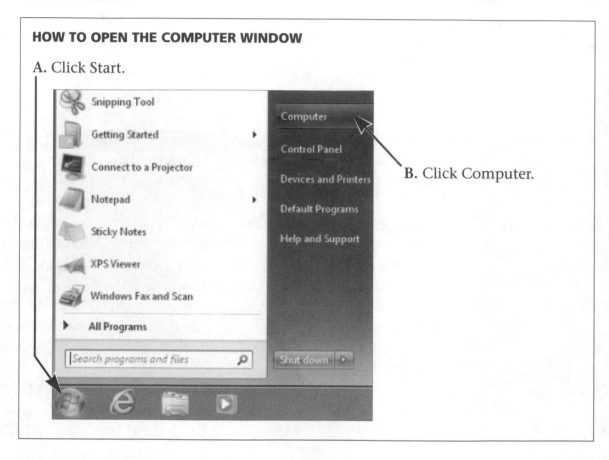

**HOW TO OPEN THE COMPUTER WINDOW**

A. Click Start.

B. Click Computer.

When the Computer window opens, you will see all the places you can save files on the computer.

**A. Navigation Pane –** Lets you select different parts of the computer

**B. Libraries –** Hold folders for different types of files

**C. Hard disk –** The permanent disk inside the computer that holds Windows and other programs

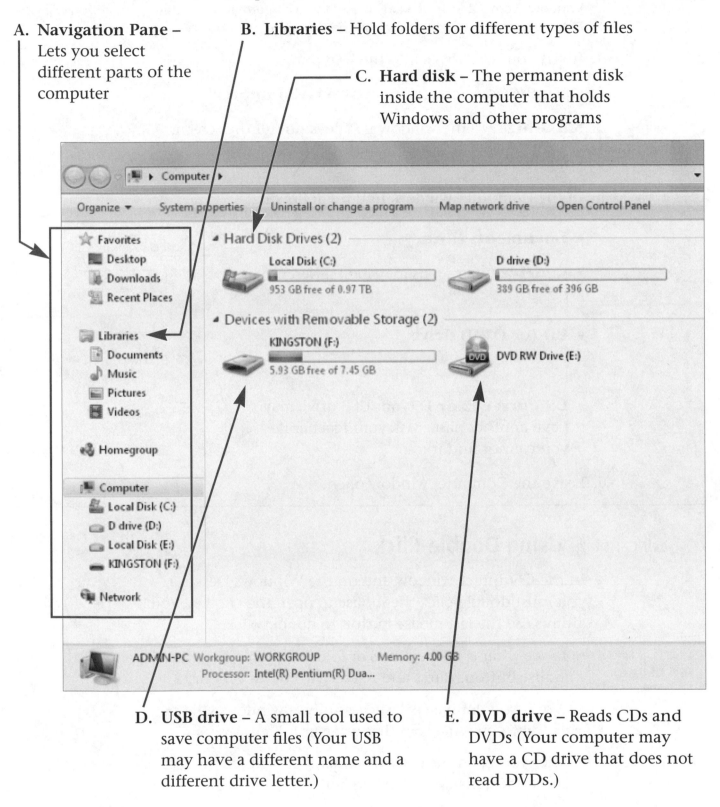

**D. USB drive –** A small tool used to save computer files (Your USB may have a different name and a different drive letter.)

**E. DVD drive –** Reads CDs and DVDs (Your computer may have a CD drive that does not read DVDs.)

**EXERCISE 6.1** **Find Places in the Computer Window**

Windows computers have many places to save information. In this exercise, you will view those different places by looking in the Computer window.

1. Insert your USB drive into the USB port.

2. Open the Computer window: **Start→Computer**.

3. **Maximize** ▣ the window if it does not fill the screen.

4. Find the **Navigation Pane**.

5. In the Computer window, find the following:

   • **Documents library:**

   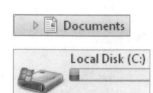

   • **C: drive** (your icons may look different):

   • **CD (or DVD) drive:**

   • **USB drive E: or F:** (your USB drive may have another name; ask your teacher if you cannot find it):

6. Leave the Computer window open.

---

**CONCEPT 6.2** **Using Double-Click**

In the Computer window and on the Windows Desktop, you must double-click the mouse to open the choices. You always use the left mouse button to double-click.

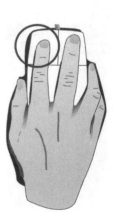

• To see what is in the drives or folders, double-click the left mouse button. (Press and release two times very fast.)

• When you double-click successfully, a window will open to show you what is in that drive or folder.

• After you open the drive or folder, you will see the files and folders inside, if there are any.

In a classroom, students usually save information to USB drives because other students will be using the same computers.

- USB drives can have many different names and different drive letters, but most computers usually use the E: or F: drive.

- To see the files on your USB drive, make sure it is inserted into the USB port. Close any new windows that open.

- Double-click the icon for your USB.

- You should see your files.

The type of icon each file has tells you in what program it will open or in what program the file was made.

  These icons tell you that the file was made in WordPad.

 A file with this icon will open in Windows Photo Viewer.

 This icon tells you that the file was made in Microsoft Word.

 Files with this icon are sound or music files.

 This is one of the icons that can be used for video files. Your computer may use a different icon.

 EXERCISE 6.2 **Use Double-Click to Open Files**

In this exercise, you will use double-click to open files. You should still be in the Computer window from the last exercise.

1. Double-click the **USB drive icon**.
   Your USB drive may have another name. Look at the files on your USB drive. Look at the icon of each file.

2. Double-click each **file icon** and look at the **title bar** of the program that opens. **Close** each program window after you look at it.

3. Click the **Back** button to return to the Computer window. Do not close the window.

## CONCEPT 6.3 **Viewing Files on a USB Drive**

There are different ways to view files in the Computer window using the Views button. (The Views button looks different in each view.)

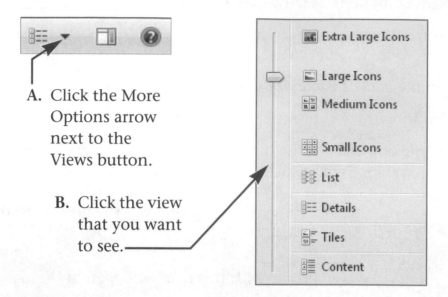

**A.** Click the More Options arrow next to the Views button.

**B.** Click the view that you want to see.

Here are some of the ways that you can view the files:

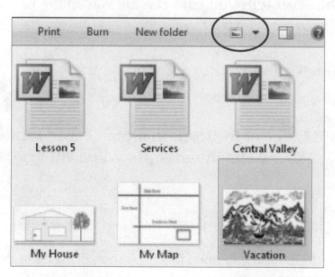

Large Icons

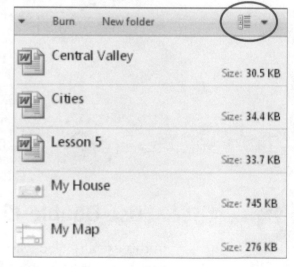

Content

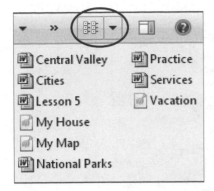

List

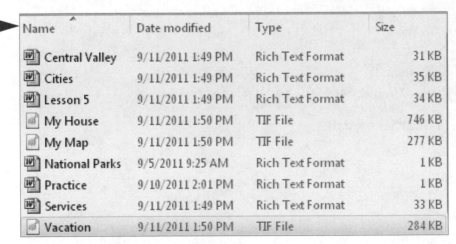

Details

The Details view shows the most information: filename, file size, file type, and more. Notice that the same files are always shown, but the way that you view them is a little different.

Sometimes it is helpful to sort your files in alphabetical order by name, by size, or by the date the file was last changed.

If you click the Name heading in Details view, you sort the files in alphabetical order by name.

| Name | Date modified | Type | Size |
|---|---|---|---|
| Central Valley | 9/11/2011 1:49 PM | Rich Text Format | 31 KB |
| Cities | 9/11/2011 1:49 PM | Rich Text Format | 35 KB |
| Lesson 5 | 9/11/2011 1:49 PM | Rich Text Format | 34 KB |
| My House | 9/11/2011 1:50 PM | TIF File | 746 KB |
| My Map | 9/11/2011 1:50 PM | TIF File | 277 KB |
| National Parks | 9/5/2011 9:25 AM | Rich Text Format | 1 KB |
| Practice | 9/10/2011 2:01 PM | Rich Text Format | 1 KB |
| Services | 9/11/2011 1:49 PM | Rich Text Format | 33 KB |
| Vacation | 9/11/2011 1:50 PM | TIF File | 284 KB |

Files in alphabetical order by name

If you click the Size heading in Detail view, you sort the files in order by size.

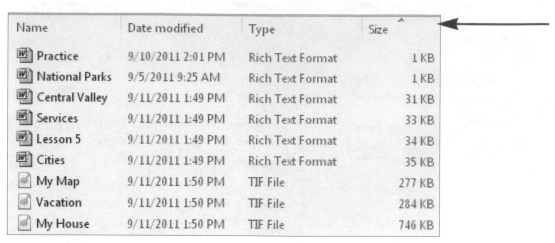

Files in order by size

If you click the Date Modified heading in Detail view, you sort the files in order by date and time.

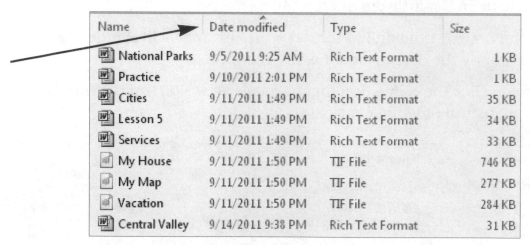

Files in order by date

**EXERCISE 6.3** **View and Sort Files**

In this exercise, you will look at the files on your USB drive. Your teacher will help you find your USB drive. Write down its name and drive letter, for example, "Removable Drive (E:)."

1. If necessary, open a Computer window with **Start→Computer**.

2. Double-click the **USB drive** to open it. You will see all of the files on your USB drive.

3. To see information about your files, click the **Views menu button ▾ →
Details**. Look at the size, type, and date of the files.

   Do not worry if you do not have the same files shown here. Your file sizes and dates will be different, too.

4. Click the **Name** heading to sort the files by name.

5. Click the **Date Modified** heading to sort the files by date.

6. Click the **Size** heading to sort the files by size.

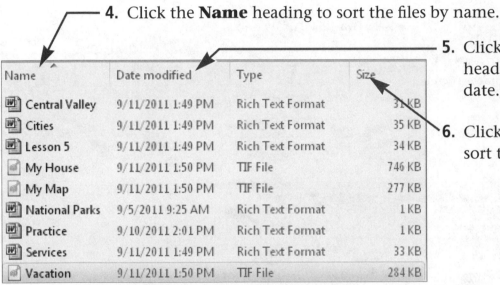

| Name | Date modified | Type | Size |
|------|---------------|------|------|
| Central Valley | 9/11/2011 1:49 PM | Rich Text Format | 31 KB |
| Cities | 9/11/2011 1:49 PM | Rich Text Format | 35 KB |
| Lesson 5 | 9/11/2011 1:49 PM | Rich Text Format | 34 KB |
| My House | 9/11/2011 1:50 PM | TIF File | 746 KB |
| My Map | 9/11/2011 1:50 PM | TIF File | 277 KB |
| National Parks | 9/5/2011 9:25 AM | Rich Text Format | 1 KB |
| Practice | 9/10/2011 2:01 PM | Rich Text Format | 1 KB |
| Services | 9/11/2011 1:49 PM | Rich Text Format | 33 KB |
| Vacation | 9/11/2011 1:50 PM | TIF File | 284 KB |

7. Click the **Back** ⊙ button to return to the Computer window.

   You will see "Computer" in the address bar.

CONCEPT 6.4 **Creating a Folder**

A folder is used to hold files and other folders in the computer. You can recognize it by its icon.

You can only create a folder when you are in one of the drives in the computer, for example, the C: drive (including in Documents and Pictures) or the USB drive.

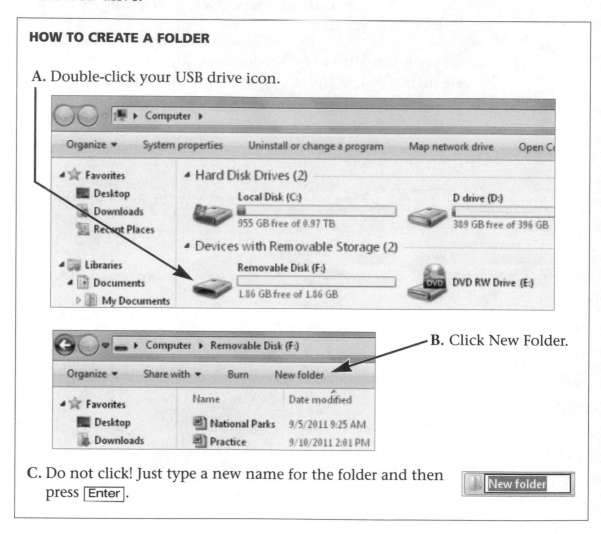

**HOW TO CREATE A FOLDER**

A. Double-click your USB drive icon.

B. Click New Folder.

C. Do not click! Just type a new name for the folder and then press Enter.

**EXERCISE 6.4** **Create Folders**

In this exercise, you will create a folder on your USB drive.

1. Double-click the **USB drive icon** to open it.

   A list of the files on your USB drive appears. In the address bar, you will see the name of your USB drive.

2. Click **New Folder**.

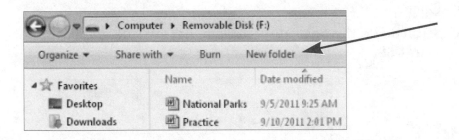

   The new folder appears.

3. *Do not* click in the New Folder box. Just type **New Files** and press ⎾Enter⏋.
   When you are finished, the folder should look like this.

   Leave the Computer window open.

# CONCEPT 6.5 Opening Files and Saving to a New Location

Sometimes you may want to save a file that you made before to a new location. One of the places you can save a file is into a different folder.

---

**HOW TO OPEN A FILE**

A. First open the program where you created the file.

B. If you are using WordPad or Paint, click the program menu button 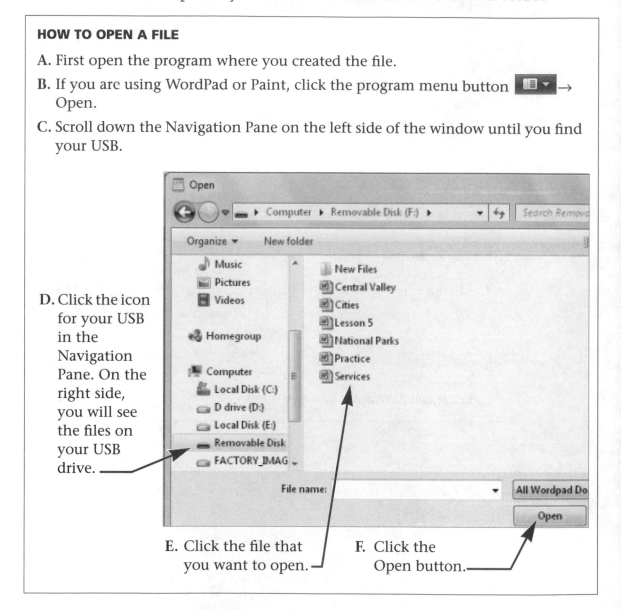 →
Open.

C. Scroll down the Navigation Pane on the left side of the window until you find
your USB.

D. Click the icon for your USB in the Navigation Pane. On the right side, you will see the files on your USB drive. ——

E. Click the file that you want to open. ┘

F. Click the Open button. ——

---

**HOW TO SAVE A FILE TO A NEW FOLDER**

A. Click the program menu button.

B. Click Save As.

C. Click the new location in the Navigation Pane or double-click the folder on
the right side of the window to open it.

   The new location will show in the address bar at the top of the window.

D. Click Save.

**EXERCISE 6.5** **Open a File and Save It to a New Location**

In this exercise, you will open a file and save it into a folder. Then you will look in the Computer window to find it.

1. Open **WordPad**.

2. Open the **Lesson 5** file from your USB drive.

   Your original (old) file opens in WordPad. Now we will save the file in a folder with a new name.

3. Click ▦▾ →**Save As**.

   The files and New Files folder on your USB drive appear on the right side.

4. Double-click the **New Files** folder to open it.

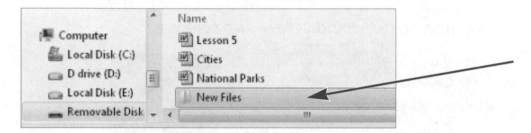

   Notice that now you can see the New Files folder name in the address bar at the top of the window. That tells you that you are inside the folder.

5. Click **Save** at the bottom of the window.

   Leave the WordPad window open.

   Now we will check to see if we really saved the file into the folder.

6. Click **Start→Computer**.

7. Double-click the icon for your **USB drive**.

8. On the right side of the window, double-click the **New Files** folder icon.

   You should see your Lesson 5 file on the right side of the Computer window. If you don't, try saving your file again and make sure to save it into the New Files folder. Follow the directions carefully.

9. Close **all windows**.

**Using Windows Help and Support**

All computers with Windows 7 come with the Help and Support program. We can type words about the computer and it will give us information.

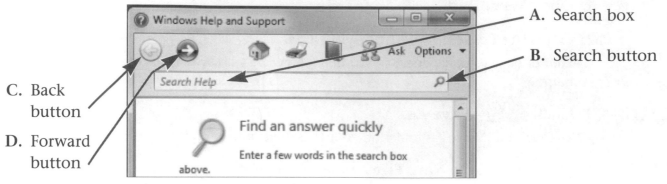

A. Search box

B. Search button

C. Back button

D. Forward button

**HOW TO USE WINDOWS HELP AND SUPPORT**

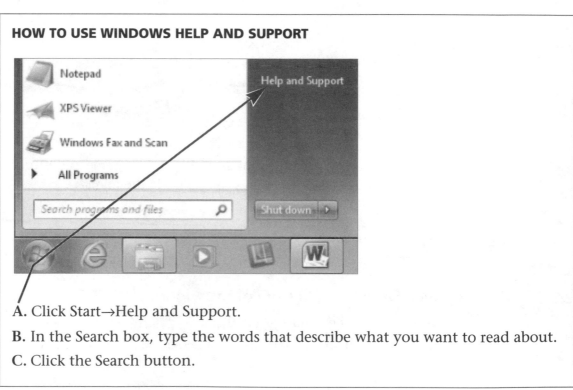

A. Click Start→Help and Support.

B. In the Search box, type the words that describe what you want to read about.

C. Click the Search button.

If you see green words, you can click them and read about what they mean.

**EXERCISE 6.6** **Search Windows Help and Support**

In this exercise, you will use Windows Help and Support find out how to make everything on your screen look larger.

1. Open Windows Help and Support: **Start→Help and Support**.

2. In the Search box, type this text:
   **make the words look larger on the screen**
   This is important for people who do not see very well.

3. Click the **Search** 🔍 button.
   You will see a list of places to click that will show you information.

4. Click the text that reads "Make the text on your screen larger or smaller."

5. Read the directions that tell how to make things look larger on your screen.

6. Close **all windows**.

# Skill Builder Exercises

**SKILL BUILDER 6.1**    ## Use Windows Help and Support

In this exercise, you will search Windows Help and Support to find information about folders in the computer.

1. Open Windows Help and Support: **Start→Help and Support**.

2. In the Search box, type **folders**.

3. Click the **Search** 🔎 button.
   You will see a list of places to click that will show you information.

4. Click the text that reads "Working with files and folders."

5. Read about files and folders. It will help you understand them better.

6. Close **all windows**.

---

**SKILL BUILDER 6.2**    ## Save a File to a New Folder

In this exercise, you will create a new file in Paint, create a new folder, and save the Paint file to the new folder. (Insert your USB drive in the computer before you start this exercise.)

1. Open the **Computer window**.

2. Scroll down the Navigation Pane on the left and click on your **USB drive**.

3. Click **New Folder**, type **Pictures** for the folder name, and press ⌷Enter⌷. Do not close the Computer window.

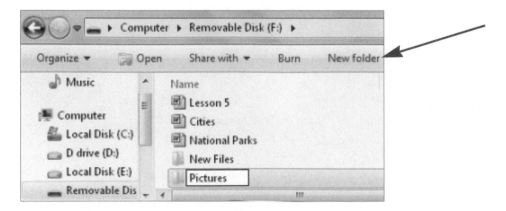

4. Open **Paint**.

5. Draw a picture of a bank close to your house.

6. Click **File→Save As**. On the left side of the window, click the icon for your **USB drive**.

7. In the **File name** box, type **Bank**.

8. Double-click the **Pictures** folder on the right side of the window and then click **Save**. (If you do not see your USB name in the address bar near the top of the window, scroll down in the Navigation Pane and click your USB icon. Then you will see your Pictures folder.)

   Now you will check to see if the file was saved in the right place.

9. Click the **Folder** icon on the taskbar.

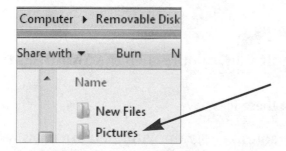

   The files and folders on your USB drive will show.

10. Double-click the **Pictures** folder.

   You should see your Bank file. Look at the icon for your Bank picture. It should look different from the icon for the WordPad files. If you do not see it, click the icon for Paint on the taskbar and save your file again.

11. Close **all windows**.

**Play a Music File**

In this exercise, you will play music files. (For this exercise, you will need to turn on the computer speakers before you start.)

1. Open the **Computer window**.

2. Click **Music** below Libraries in the Navigation Pane.

You may see some music files now.

3. If you do not see any music files, double-click the **Sample Music** folder to open it.

   Look at the type of icon that these files have.

4. Double-click **any file**. A sound program will open and you will hear the music.

5. When you are finished listening to the music, click the **Close** button for the sound program.

6. You can listen to other songs by double-clicking the files.

7. When you are finished listening, close **all windows**.

**Personal Project: Use Paint, WordPad, and a Computer Window**

In this exercise, you will use Paint, WordPad, and a Computer window. (You will need your USB drive in the computer before you start this exercise.)

1. Open **Paint**. Create a picture of a park with trees and flowers.

2. **Save** the file as **Park** to your USB drive. Then, save the file as **Park2** in the **Pictures** folder that you made in Skill Builder 6.2.

3. Open **WordPad**. Type the name of your new park and then center it on the page.

4. On the left, type five sentences about what you would like to have at your park.

5. Save the file as **Park Details** to your **USB drive**.

6. Open the **Computer window**.

7. Double-click the icon for your **USB drive**.

8. Click the **Views menu button ▾→Details** to see the files in Details view.

9. Click the **Date** heading once to sort the files by date.
   Your new files show at the top of the list.

10. Click the **Name** heading to put the files in order by name.

# Conversation

## Paired Conversation

With a partner, take turns reading the A and B parts of the conversation.

| | |
|---|---|
| Student A | Hi. You look like you need help. |
| Student B | Yes, I do. |
| Student A | What's the problem? |
| Student B | I click the icon, but nothing happens. |
| Student A | Oh, you have to double-click it. |
| Student B | I want to see the files that I saved on my USB drive. |
| Student A | Okay. First you have to open a Computer window. |
| Student B | How do I do that? |
| Student A | Click the Start button and then click Computer. It is on the right side of the Start menu. |
| Student B | Okay. Now a Computer window is open, but I still don't see my files. |
| Student A | You will see them soon. Double-click your USB drive icon. |
| Student B | Now I see them! Why do some of them have little Ws on their icons? |
| Student A | Well, that is because they were made in WordPad. |
| Student B | Why do we make folders? |
| Student A | I like to put my files into folders so they are more organized. It is like putting my clothes in dresser drawers at home. |
| Student B | The teacher said that we will be able to play music files today. |
| Student A | That sounds like fun! |

# Using the Internet

## LEARNING OBJECTIVES

After studying this lesson, you will be able to:

### Computer Objectives

- Open and use Internet Explorer

- Use a search engine to find information

- Type an Internet address to go to a website

- Apply for a job online

### Language Objectives

- Use vocabulary words to describe opening and using Internet Explorer

- Describe actions to take when using a search engine

- Use appropriate verbs when describing how to find information on the Internet

- Talk about typing addresses in the address bar

- Tell a partner how to go to a website

*Student Resources labyrinthelab.com/esl3*

 **Vocabulary**

# Picture Dictionary – Nouns

A noun is the name of a person, place, or thing. The following nouns are introduced in this lesson:

| | | |
|---|---|---|
| **1.** Internet  | **2.** Modem  | **3.** Link  |
| **4.** Internet connection  | **5.** Scroll bar  | **6.** Website  |

1. **Internet** – Computers from all over the world connected so they can communicate

2. **Modem** – A tool that connects your computer to the Internet

3. **Link** – An object or text that takes you from one web page to another when you click on it

4. **Internet connection** – The system that lets you make contact with the Internet

5. **Scroll bar** – The bar that lets you move to other parts of a web page

6. **Website** – A place on the Internet where you can find information by using a search engine or an Internet address

# Picture Dictionary – Nouns (continued)

| | |
|---|---|
| **7.** Internet address  | **8.** Web browser 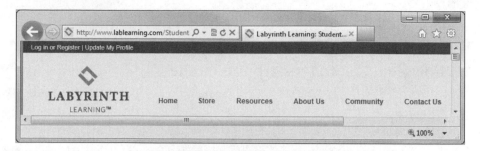 |
| **9.** Simulation  | **10.** ISP  |
| **11.** Homepage 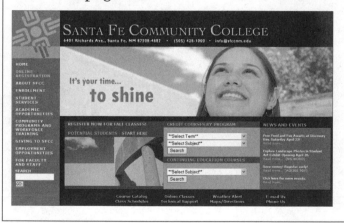 | **12.** Search engine  |

**7. Internet address** – The unique address for each web page

**8. Web browser** – Software that lets you connect to the Internet

**9. Simulation** – An exercise that is not real; it is planned ahead of time, with all the possibilities already set

**10. ISP (Internet Service Provider)** – A company that gives you a connection to the Internet; usually, you have to pay money for this service

**11. Homepage** – The page that appears when you open Internet Explorer or another web browser

**12. Search engine** – A website you can use to look for things on the Internet

# Computer Verbs

A verb tells an action or what a subject is or does. The following verbs are introduced in this lesson:

| VERB | MEANING | EXAMPLE |
|---|---|---|
| 1. Browse | To look around on the Internet | I need some ideas for a gift, so I'm going to browse the Internet to see what I can find. |
| 2. Connect | To make contact with the Internet | I will connect to the Internet to find the information I need. |
| 3. Search | To look for information on a specific topic on the Internet | I am writing a book report. I will search the Internet for facts about my topic. |
| 4. Visit | To look at a website | I have a few minutes to visit my favorite news website. |

# Concepts and Exercises

## What Is the Internet?

The Internet is millions of computers from all parts of the world connected so they can communicate. To join the Internet, you must have an Internet connection. You get one by signing up with an Internet service provider (ISP). For most types of connections, you need a modem.

Internet      Internet Service      Users
Provider

## Types of Internet Connections

There are different ways to connect to the Internet. They have different speeds and costs. For each type of connection, you should be able to find a few different ISPs in your area.

- **Dial-up** – This uses a regular telephone line to connect to the Internet. Dial-up costs less money than other types of connections. It is the slowest type of connection.

- **Cable** – This connection uses the same cable as cable television.

- **DSL** – You must have a special telephone line to use this type of connection.

- **Satellite** – A cable connects you to a satellite dish. The dish communicates with a satellite for Internet access.

- **Wi-Fi** – Wireless networking sends the Internet data through the air. No wires or cables are needed.

**Using Internet Explorer**

You need special software on your computer to connect to the Internet. This special software is called an Internet browser. Many people use Internet Explorer as their browser.

**A. Back and Forward buttons** – These buttons help you move among websites.

**B. Address bar** – In this bar, you can see the Internet address of the website you are visiting. You can also click in the address bar and type the address of a website you want to visit.

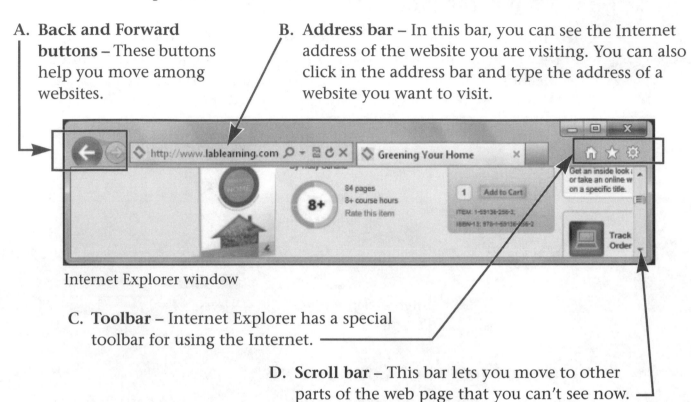

Internet Explorer window

**C. Toolbar** – Internet Explorer has a special toolbar for using the Internet.

**D. Scroll bar** – This bar lets you move to other parts of the web page that you can't see now.

**Start Internet Explorer**

In this exercise, you will start Internet Explorer.

1. Click the **Internet Explorer** 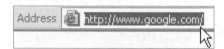 button on the taskbar. (If you do not see it, you can click **Start→All Programs→Internet Explorer**.)

   The homepage will open. A homepage is the first page Internet Explorer shows when you start the program.

2. Point with your mouse (don't click) on the Back button. Watch for the ScreenTip to come up.

3. Put your mouse on other icons. Watch for the ScreenTips to show on each one. (The icons that have words showing do not have ScreenTips.)

   Leave the Internet Explorer window open.

---

CONCEPT 7.3 **Using the Address Bar**

When you click in the address bar once, the address that is there becomes highlighted.

Then you can type in a new address. You do not have to use Backspace or Delete if the address is highlighted.

EXERCISE 7.3 **Go to a Website**

In this exercise, you will type an address in the address bar. Internet Explorer should still be open.

1. Click in the white part of the **address bar** and see that the address is highlighted.

2. Type **www.yahoo.com** and press Enter to go to the new website.

3. Take a minute to look at this website.

4. Click the **Back** button to go back to where you were when you started.

   Remember, the place where you start when you open Internet Explorer is called the homepage.

CONCEPT 7.4 **Using a Search Engine**

A search engine is a website made to look for things on the Internet. Google is one of the many search engines you can use.

**A.** This is the name of the search engine.

**B.** Links usually look like words or pictures. When you click them, you go to another web page. You know that something is a link when you put your mouse pointer on it and the pointer changes to a hand symbol 🖑.

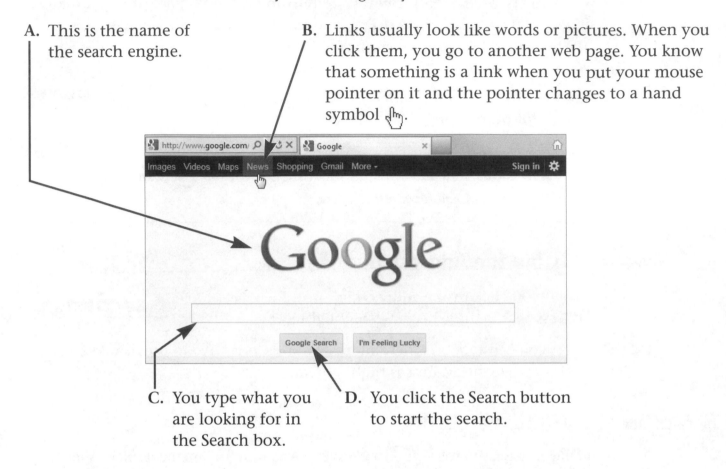

**C.** You type what you are looking for in the Search box.

**D.** You click the Search button to start the search.

**EXERCISE 7.4** **Search with Google**

 In this exercise, you will use a simulation of a search engine to practice finding information.

1. Start **Internet Explorer** if it is not already open.

2. Click once in the **address bar**. Type **labyrinthelab.com/esl3** and tap ⌈Enter⌉.

3. From the left navigation bar, click **Lesson 7 Using the Internet** and then click **Exercise 7.4: Search with Google**.

   You will see a simulation of Google appear. Now you will do a search.

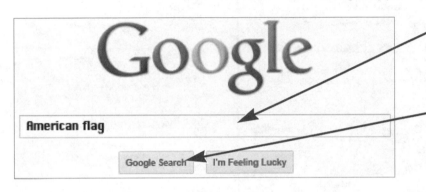

4. Click in the **Search box** and type **American flag**.

5. Click the **Google Search** button.

Google displays the search results. Notice how many there are.

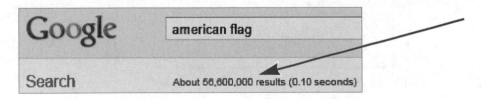

6. Click the green **Back to Course** link that is under the WebSim window.

**Search Results**

When the search engine gives you the results, take a few minutes to look at them. You should decide which ones have what you are searching for. Sometimes you have to look at a few to get what you want. You can add more words to your search if you cannot find what you are searching for.

A. Web page title

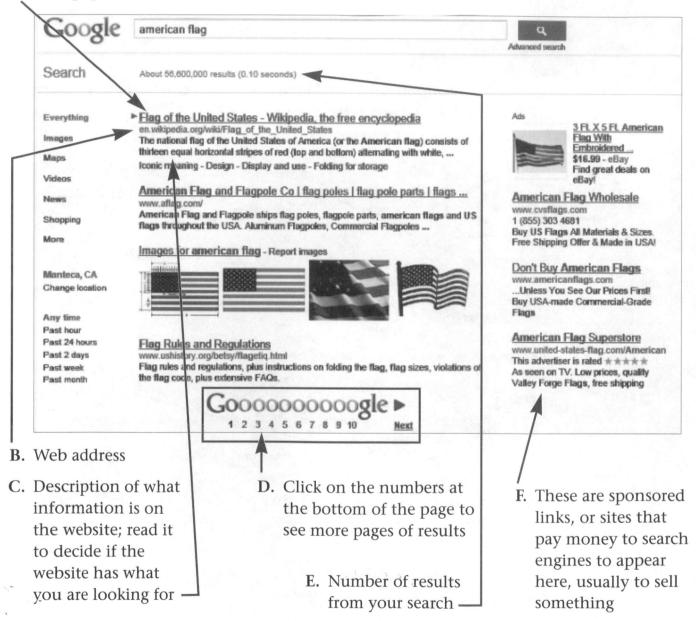

B. Web address

C. Description of what information is on the website; read it to decide if the website has what you are looking for

D. Click on the numbers at the bottom of the page to see more pages of results

E. Number of results from your search

F. These are sponsored links, or sites that pay money to search engines to appear here, usually to sell something

## Other Search Engines

These results are only from one search engine. They change every day and will look different when you use a different search engine, like Yahoo.com or Bing.com.

# Using Scroll Bars

Scroll bars are used to move around in a window. They let you go to parts of the web page that do not show because it is too tall or too wide to fit on one page. The scroll bars let you move around to see the rest of the web page.

**A.** Vertical scroll bar

**B.** Horizontal scroll bar

You cannot see the whole web page without scrolling.

**A.** Click the top arrow of the vertical scroll bar to go up.

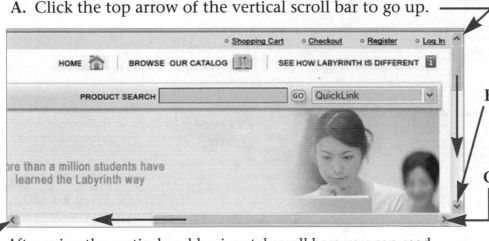

**B.** Click the bottom arrow of the vertical scroll bar to go down.

**C.** Click the right arrow of the horizontal scroll bar to move to the right.

After using the vertical and horizontal scroll bars you can read the web page.

**D.** Click the left arrow of the horizontal scroll bar to move to the left.

### EXERCISE 7.5  Go to a Search Result

In this exercise, you will use a simulation of a search engine to practice finding information.

1. If necessary, type **labyrinthelab.com/es13** into the address bar of your web browser and tap [Enter].

2. If necessary, click **Lesson 7** in the left navigation bar and then click **Lesson 7 Using the Internet**. To access the WebSim, click **Exercise 7.5: Go to a Search Result**.

   When you decide what link has the information you are looking for, click on its web page title.

#### View a Search Result

3. Click the **scroll bar** to see more search results.

4. Click the **top arrow** to scroll back up to find the Wikipedia search result. (Wikipedia is a free online encyclopedia.)

5. Click on the **Flag of the United States - Wikipedia, the Free Encyclopedia** link.

The Wikipedia web page about the flag of the United States appears.

## Go to a Web Page Using a Link

**6.** Point at the link for the **50 states**, and notice how the mouse pointer turns into a hand. This tells you it is a link.

**7.** Click on the link for the **50 states**.

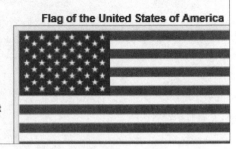

### Flag of the United States

From Wikipedia, the free encyclopedia

*"American Flag" redirects here. For the Arizona ghost town, see American Flag, Arizona.*

*"Flag of Columbia" redirects here. For the flag of the South American country, see Flag of Colombia.*

The national **flag of the United States of America** (or the **American flag**) consists of thirteen equal horizontal stripes of red (top and bottom) alternating with white, with a blue rectangle in the canton (referred to specifically as the "union") bearing fifty small, white, five-pointed stars arranged in nine offset horizontal rows of six stars (top and bottom) alternating with rows of five stars. The fifty stars on the flag represent the 50 states and the 13 stripes represent the thirteen colonies that rebelled against the British monarchy and became the f  U.S. state  he Union.[1]

**Flag of the United States of America**

You will see the U.S. states web page appear.

### U.S. state

From Wikipedia, the free encyclopedia

A **U.S. state** (abbreviation of **United States state**) is any one of the 50 federated states of the United States of America that share sovereignty with the federal government. Because of this shared sovereignty, an American is a citizen both of the federal entity and of his or her state of domicile.[1] Four states use the official title of *commonwealth* rather than *state*. State citizenship is flexible and no government approval is required to move between states (with the exception of convicts on parole).

**8.** Click the **Back** button two times to go back to the Google search results. Now you can look at other search results or start a new search.

**9.** Click the **Close** button to close Internet Explorer.

# Skill Builder Exercises

**Go to Another Website**

In this exercise, you will go to a website using the address bar.

1. Click the **Internet Explorer** button on the taskbar. (If you do not see it, you can click **Start→All Programs→Internet Explorer**.)

2. Click once in the **address bar**. Then, type **answers.com** and press [Enter].

3. Click on any of the links that look interesting to you.
Watch for the mouse pointer to change to the hand before you click.

4. Click the **Back** ◉ button to return to the homepage.

**Search the Internet**

In this exercise, you will search using Google.com.

1. Click in the **address bar**. Then, type **www.google.com** and press Enter .

2. Click in the **Search box**, type **US citizenship test questions**, and press Enter .

3. Look at the results that come up. Read the descriptions carefully.

4. **Scroll down** to see more search results.

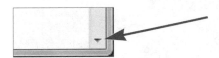

5. Pick out one site you think has the information you are looking for, and click on its web page title.

6. When the web page opens, look to see if it shows what you want.

7. When you finish reading, click the **Back** button.

8. Try one of the other results by clicking on its title.

9. When you find a web page that shows some of the citizenship questions, read them.

## SKILL BUILDER 7.3 **Fill Out a Job Application Online**

In this exercise, you will use a simulation to see what it is like to fill out a job application form on the Internet.

1. If necessary, type **labyrinthelab.com/es13** into the **address bar** of your web browser and tap Enter.

2. From the left navigation bar, click **Lesson 7**. Click **Lesson 7 Using the Internet** and then click **Skill Builder 7.3: Fill Out a Job Application Online**.

   A web page appears with a simulated form to fill out. No information will actually be sent. This is just for practice.

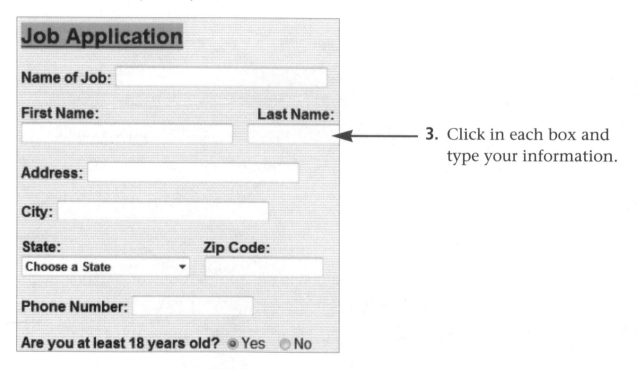

3. Click in each box and type your information.

4. Scroll down to enter all of your information. When you see a drop-down box with an arrow next to it, click the arrow then click your answer. Sometimes you can scroll down to find more choices. If you see circles or boxes next to an answer, click in the circle or box to choose.

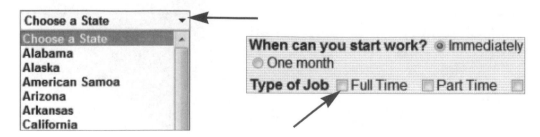

5. When you are finished, click [ Submit ].

If this were a real online application, the Submit button would send your information to the company where you are applying. In this simulation, your information will not go anywhere.

6. Close **Internet Explorer**.

---

**Personal Project: Search for a State Governor**

In this exercise, you will use the Google.com search engine to find information about someone in your state.

1. Use **Google.com** to search for information about the governor of the state where you live.

2. Click on some of the web page titles to see what information appears.

3. Print one of the pages about the governor: Click the **Tools** ⚙ button on the Internet Explorer toolbar, click **Print**, and then click **Print** again.

---

# Conversation

## Paired Conversation

With a partner, take turns reading the A and B parts of the conversation.

| | |
|---|---|
| Student A | I'm a new student. |
| Student B | Welcome to our classroom! |
| Student A | I heard that today's class is about the Internet. |
| Student B | That's right. |
| Student A | Which websites will we visit? |
| Student B | I'm not sure. We'll have to use a search engine. |
| Student A | Is that what you use to look for things on the Internet? |
| Student B | That's right. |
| Student A | Well, let's visit an interesting website. |
| Student B | I know! Let's go to our school's homepage first. |
| Student A | That's a great idea. Let's connect to it now. |
| Student B | Well, let's type in the Internet address for our school. |
| Student A | Okay. Now what do I do? |
| Student B | We can use the links to go to the pages we want. |
| Student A | Thanks. Now I want to browse the Internet. |
| Student B | You'll have to wait. We have to do a simulation exercise first. |
| Student A | Okay. |
| Student B | Later, we can search for other interesting subjects. |

# Working with Email

## LEARNING OBJECTIVES

After studying this lesson, you will be able to:

**Computer Objectives**

- Sign in to email and send a message

- Reply to an email message

- Forward a message

**Language Objectives**

- Use vocabulary words to describe signing in to email

- Use computer verbs to describe actions taken with email messages

- Describe how to reply to and forward a message

*Student Resources labyrinthelab.com/esl3*

 **Vocabulary**

# Picture Dictionary – Nouns

A noun is the name of a person, place, or thing. The following nouns are introduced in this lesson:

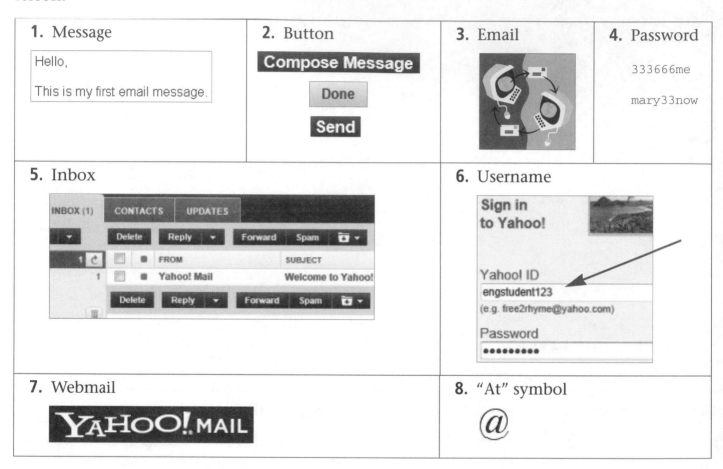

| | | | |
|---|---|---|---|
| **1.** Message | **2.** Button | **3.** Email | **4.** Password |
| Hello,<br><br>This is my first email message. | Compose Message<br>Done<br>Send | | 333666me<br><br>mary33now |
| **5.** Inbox | | **6.** Username | |
| INBOX (1)  CONTACTS  UPDATES<br>Delete  Reply  Forward  Spam<br>1  FROM  SUBJECT<br>1  Yahoo! Mail  Welcome to Yahoo!<br>Delete  Reply  Forward  Spam | | Sign in to Yahoo!<br>Yahoo! ID<br>engstudent123<br>(e.g. free2rhyme@yahoo.com)<br>Password<br>•••••••• | |
| **7.** Webmail | | **8.** "At" symbol | |
| YAHOO! MAIL | | @ | |

1. **Message** – Information that you type and send to another person using email

2. **Button** – A small rectangle that completes an action when you click it

3. **Email (Electronic mail)** – A way to send information from one computer to another

4. **Password** – A personal word or combination of letters and numbers that lets you get into your email

5. **Inbox** – A page in your email that lists all the messages you have received

6. **Username** – The name you choose for your personal email account

7. **Webmail** – An email service that allows you to reach your email account from computers other than your own

8. **"At" symbol** – The character that is included in email addresses between the username and the email provider name

# Computer Verbs

A verb tells an action or what a subject is or does. The following verbs are introduced in this lesson:

| VERB | MEANING | EXAMPLE |
|------|---------|---------|
| 1. Compose | To write a message | I'll compose a message explaining my question and send it to my teacher. |
| 2. Send | To transmit a message from your email to another person's email | I will send a message to my mother tomorrow. |
| 3. Forward | To send a message that you received to another person | I received a wonderful message from Mary. I am going to forward it to Jane, so she can read it, too. |
| 4. Reply | To answer a message that you received | My friend sent me a message saying that she is sick. I need to reply and ask her if she needs anything. |

# Concepts and Exercises

CONCEPT 8.1 **About Email**

Email is a fast and easy way to communicate with people in all places in the world that have the Internet. You must have an email address and Internet access to use email. All Internet service providers give you an email address when you sign up.

- An email address must have three parts. It cannot have any spaces.

  Sample email address: student@msn.com

| USERNAME | AT SYMBOL | EMAIL SERVICE PROVIDER |
|----------|-----------|------------------------|
| student  | @         | msn.com                |

- You will be using webmail in this book. Webmail is useful because you can use it from any computer in the world that has Internet access.

- Many companies on the Internet offer free webmail. You can use a search engine to find the companies that do. Yahoo! Mail is a popular webmail service.

## Getting an Email Account

When you get an email account, you must pick a username and a password.

- The username is the special name that you use to access your email.

- The password must be entered to keep your email safe. No one can read your email unless they have your username and your password.

After you get an email account, you can send and receive email.

**A Note About The WebSims in This Lesson** As you work through the WebSims in this lesson, watch for a button that reads "Click here to continue." You will need to click this button to restart the WebSim at certain points.

`Click here to continue`

**Sign In to Email**

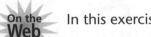

**On the Web**

In this exercise, you will use a simulation to practice email before you try the real thing.

1. Click the **Internet Explorer**  button on the taskbar at the bottom of your screen.

2. Click once in the **address bar**. Type **labyrinthelab.com/esl3** and tap Enter.

3. From the left navigation bar, click **Lesson 8**. Click **Lesson 8 Working with Email** and then click **Exercise 8.1: Sign In to Email**.

   You will see the Yahoo! simulation page.

4. Click the **Mail** link. It may be on the left side or the right side of the page.

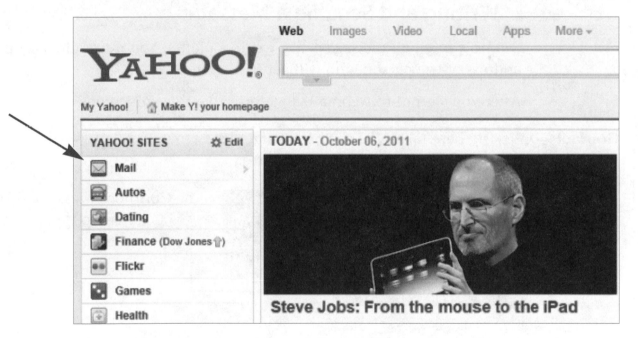

Now you will sign in.

 **TIP!** In this and other WebSims in this lesson, remember to be on the lookout for the "Click here to continue" button. Click the button to make the WebSim start again.

## Sign In

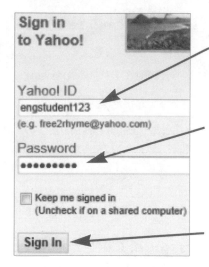

5. Click in the **Yahoo! ID** box and type **engstudent123** as your account name.

6. Type **learnmail** in the **Password** box. You will see dots instead of your password. This is to help keep your password secret.

7. Click the **Sign In** button.

8. Click the green **Back to Course** link that is under the WebSim window.

---

### CONCEPT 8.2 **Writing and Sending a Message**

Sending an email message is like writing a letter. You must add the email address of the person who will get the letter.

After you sign in to webmail, a window like this will come up.

**A. Contacts** – Clicking here takes you to your contact list, where you enter and keep people's email addresses.

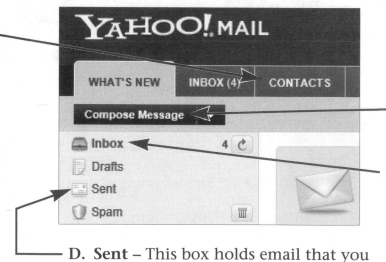

**B. Compose Message** – You click here to type a new message.

**C. Inbox** – This box holds the email sent to you. You click it to open it.

**D. Sent** – This box holds email that you have already sent. Click it to open it.

**Type and Send an Email Message**

In this exercise, you will create (compose) and send a new email message.

1. If necessary, type **labyrinthelab.com/esl3** into the address bar of your web browser and tap [Enter].

2. If necessary, click **Lesson 8** in the left navigation bar and then click **Lesson 8 Working with Email**. To access the WebSim, click **Exercise 8.2: Type and Send an Email Message**.

3. Click the **Compose Message** button.

You will see a screen that lets you type a message.

4. Type the email address of the person you are sending the message to in the **To** box.

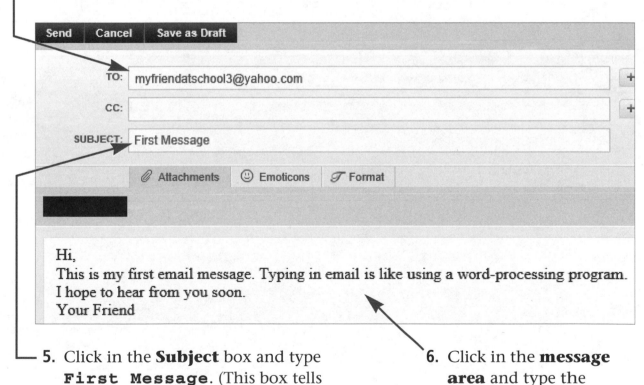

5. Click in the **Subject** box and type **First Message**. (This box tells what your message is about.)

6. Click in the **message area** and type the message shown here.

**7.** Click **Send** .

Yahoo! Mail will tell you that the message was sent.

**8.** Click **Done** to go back to the email window.

**9.** Click the green **Back to Course** link that is under the WebSim window.

---

CONCEPT 8.3 **Working with Contacts**

Contacts is an address book in Yahoo! with a list of names and email addresses. Yahoo! lets you save names and email addresses in your Contacts address book to use again later.

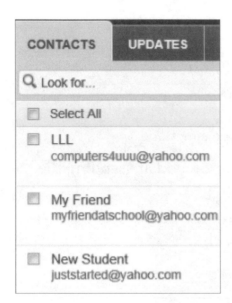

# EXERCISE 8.3  Add a Person to Contacts

In this exercise, you will add someone to your Contacts list.

1. If necessary, type **labyrinthelab.com/esl3** into the address bar of your web browser and tap ⏎Enter⏎.

2. If necessary, click **Lesson 8** in the left navigation bar and then click **Lesson 8 Working with Email**. To access the WebSim, click **Exercise 8.3: Add a Person to Contacts**.

   Now you will save an address so you do not have to type it again for future email messages.

3. Click the **Contacts** tab.

4. Click **New Contact**.

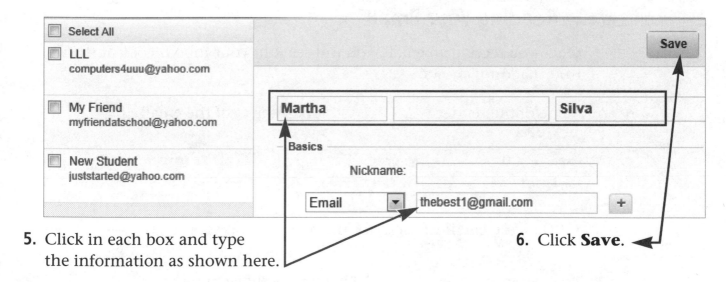

5. Click in each box and type the information as shown here.

6. Click **Save**.

   You will now see Martha Silva in your Contacts list.

7. Click the ⌷INBOX⌷ tab to go back to the Inbox.

Let's look at the email you sent.

8. To see that you have sent the last email, click **Sent** on the left side of the window.

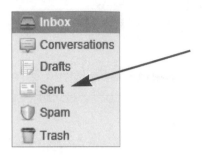

9. Click the **subject** of the message to read it.

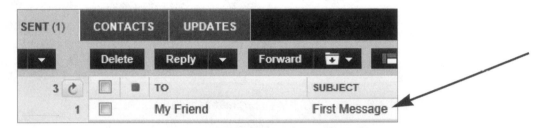

10. Click the green **Back to Course** link that is under the WebSim window.

---

CONCEPT 8.4 **Reading Your Email**

Once you receive an email, you will see it in your Inbox. Look at the information it shows.

A. Name of the sender        B. Subject of the email

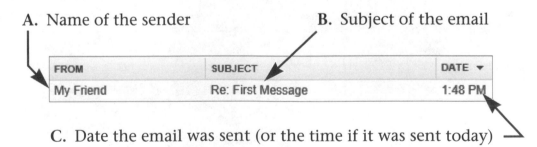

C. Date the email was sent (or the time if it was sent today)

You can read the email by clicking on the subject line.

## EXERCISE 8.4 Check for New Email

In this exercise, you will check your mail, open a message, and print a message.

1. If necessary, type **labyrinthelab.com/esl3** into the address bar of your web browser and tap Enter.

2. If necessary, click **Lesson 8** in the left navigation bar and then click **Lesson 8 Working with Email**. To access the WebSim, click **Exercise 8.4: Check for New Email**.

3. Click the INBOX tab to look at your email.

    A new email message appears in the list.

4. Look at the name of the person who sent the message.

5. Look at the date the message was sent. (If the time shows, then it was sent today.)

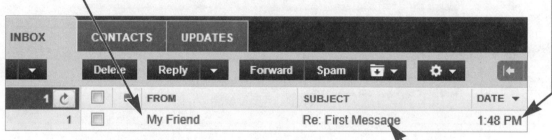

6. Click the **subject** of the first message to read it.

    The message appears on the screen.

7. If you want to print the message, hold down the Ctrl key and press P. Then, click **OK** or **Print**. You must follow these printing instructions because this is a simulation.

    Leave the message open on the screen.

8. Click the green **Back to Course** link that is under the WebSim window.

## CONCEPT 8.5  Replying to a Message

When you want to answer a message, you reply to it.

**Reply** When you click the Reply button, Yahoo! takes you to a new window so you can type an answer to the email that was sent to you. You will see your cursor blinking at the top of the message box.

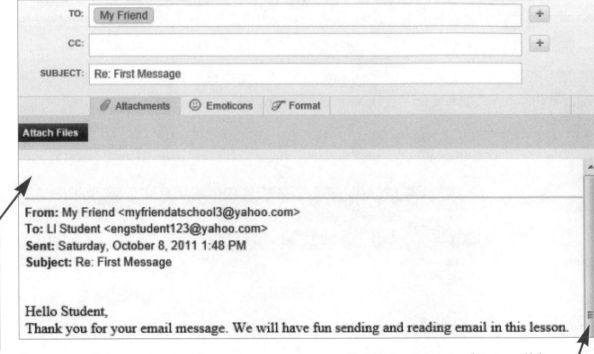

**A.** You type the answer to the message above the message that was sent to you.

**B.** You can use the scroll bar to see the rest of the original message.

## EXERCISE 8.5  Reply to an Email Message

**On the Web** In this exercise, you will send a reply to the email message you just opened.

1. If necessary, type **labyrinthelab.com/esl3** into the address bar of your web browser and tap ⌷Enter⌷.

2. If necessary, click **Lesson 8** in the left navigation bar and then click **Lesson 8 Working with Email**. To access the WebSim, click **Exercise 8.5: Reply to an Email Message**.

3. Click **Reply** to answer the message.

   The window opens for you to type your answer.

### Type a Reply

4. Highlight the text RE: First Message in the Subject box and type **Replying** to replace the old text.

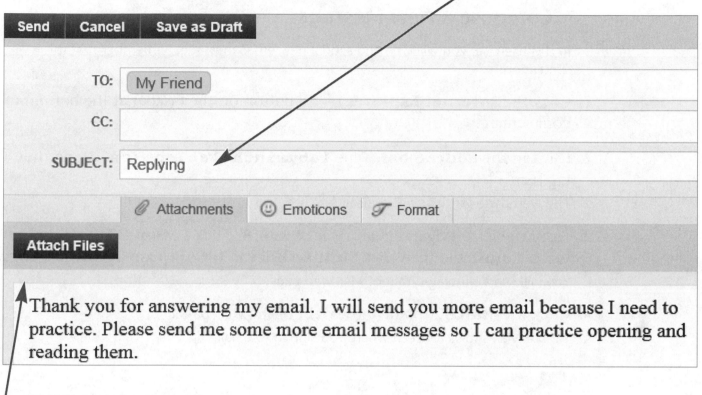

5. Click at the top of the message box and type your reply message.
   It is not necessary to delete the other text.

6. Click **Send** above the email message.
   Yahoo! shows that your message was sent.

7. Click the green **Back to Course** link that is under the WebSim window.

# Skill Builder Exercises

**Compose a New Message**

In this exercise, you will type and send a new email message. Remember that this is a simulation.

1. Click the **Internet Explorer** button on the taskbar at the bottom of your screen.

2. Click in the **address bar**. Type `labyrinthelab.com/es13` and then tap `Enter`.

   The web page for this book appears.

3. From the left navigation bar, click **Lesson 8**. Click **Lesson 8 Working with Email** and then click **Skill Builder 8.1: Compose a New Message**.

   You will see a simulated Yahoo! Mail web page.

4. Click the **Mail** button near the right of the web page.

   Yahoo! Mail shows a screen where you sign in to email.

5. Type this Yahoo ID and Password in the proper boxes:
   Yahoo! ID: **engstudent123**
   Password: **learnemail**

6. Click the **Sign In** button.

7. Click the **Compose Message** button on the left side of the window.

   A new message appears on the screen.

8. Click in the **To** box and type **mydoctor789@yahoo.com** as the address.

9. Click in the **Subject** box and type `Flu Shots` as the subject of the message.

10. Click in the **message screen** and type a message asking your doctor when he will be giving flu shots.

11. Click **Send**.

    Yahoo! Mail will show you a message telling you that your message was sent.

12. Click **Done** to go to the Inbox.

13. Click the **Sent** folder in the folders box on the left side of the window.

14. Click **Flu Shots** link in the Subject column of the Sent folder.

    Yahoo! Mail will show your message.

15. Click the green **Back to Course** link that is under the WebSim window.

# Check for New Email and Reply to an Email

In this exercise, you will check for new email and reply to a new email message.

1. If necessary, type **labyrinthelab.com/es13** into the address bar of your web browser and tap Enter .

2. If necessary, click **Lesson 8** in the left navigation bar and then click **Lesson 8 Working with Email**. To access the WebSim, click **Skill Builder 8.2: Check for New Email and Reply to an Email**.

## Check for Incoming Messages

3. Click the INBOX tab in the upper-left corner of the web page.

4. Click the **Re: Flu Shots** link at the top of the Subject column of the Inbox message list.

The reply to your Flu Shots message appears.

"Re:" means that this is a reply to the email that you sent.

## Reply to a Message

5. Click Reply at the top of the message. See that the To and Subject boxes are already filled in for you.

6. **Type a reply** to the message, thanking your doctor for sending the information.

7. Highlight the text **RE: Flu Shots** in the Subject box and type **Thank you** to replace the old text.

Now the subject should read *Thank you*.

8. Click Send and then click Done .

### Check for New Messages

9. Click the INBOX tab in the upper-left corner of the web page.

10. Click the link to your new message from your doctor in the Inbox.

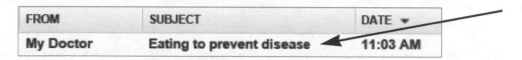

| FROM | SUBJECT | DATE ▼ |
|------|---------|--------|
| My Doctor | Eating to prevent disease | 11:03 AM |

11. Click the green **Back to Course** link that is under the WebSim window.

---

**SKILL BUILDER 8.3**    # Forward a Message

 Sometimes you will want to send an email message that you received to someone else. In this exercise, you will forward the message from your doctor to a friend.

1. If necessary, type **labyrinthelab.com/es13** into the address bar of your web browser and tap Enter.

2. If necessary, click **Lesson 8** in the left navigation bar and then click **Lesson 8 Working with Email**. To access the WebSim, click **Skill Builder 8.3: Forward a Message**.

3. Click **Forward** near the top of the message.

4. In the **To** box, type the email address **computers4uuu@yahoo.com**.

5. Click at the top of the message box and then type this message:

   **I thought you might like to read this information about healthy eating.** Enter
   Enter
   **[Your Name]** Enter

6. Click **Send**.

**7.** Click the [INBOX] tab to display the Inbox.

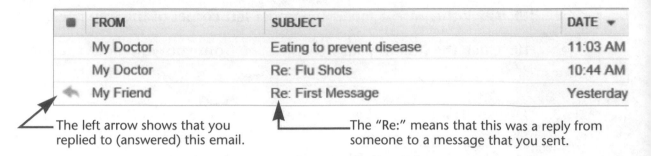

| ■ | FROM | SUBJECT | DATE ▼ |
|---|------|---------|--------|
| | My Doctor | Eating to prevent disease | 11:03 AM |
| | My Doctor | Re: Flu Shots | 10:44 AM |
| ← | My Friend | Re: First Message | Yesterday |

The left arrow shows that you replied to (answered) this email.

The "Re:" means that this was a reply from someone to a message that you sent.

**8.** Close the **web browser window**.

---

SKILL BUILDER 8.4    **Personal Project: Sign Up for Webmail**

In this exercise, you will sign up for real webmail on Yahoo! It is free and will look like the simulations you have been using.

**!NOTE!** The Yahoo! Mail website may not look exactly like the pictures on this page.

**1.** Open **Internet Explorer** and click in the **address bar**. Then, type **www.yahoo.com** and tap [Enter].

**2.** Click the **Mail** button.

**3.** On the bottom part of the window, click **Create a New Account**.

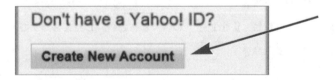

Yahoo! displays a web page with a form where you can create a new webmail account.

**4.** Type your information in each box.

You may have to ask your teacher or a friend for help if you do not understand what you should put in each box.

Type the code shown [                    ]    ⟳ Try a new code

By clicking the "Create My Account" button below, I certify that I have read and agree to the Yahoo! Terms of Service, Yahoo! Privacy Policy and Communications Terms of Service, and to receive account related communications from Yahoo! electronically. To deliver product features, relevant advertising and abuse protection, Yahoo!'s automated systems scan and analyze all email, IM and other communications content.

**Create My Account**

**5.** In the box, type the numbers or letters shown above it. Then, click **Create My Account**.

If you did not complete something correctly, Yahoo! will tell you and you can fix the problem. If everything is complete, Yahoo! will show a "Congratulations" message.

# Congratulations
A confirmation message was sent to you via email.

**Below are your account details**   🖶 Print Account Details

You will need this information to sign in to Yahoo! and to reset your password in case you forget it. Please print and keep this information in a safe place for future reference.

**6.** Write down your **username and password** because you will need them to sign in to your email.

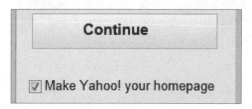

**Continue**

☑ Make Yahoo! your homepage

**7.** Click the checkbox next to **Make Yahoo! Your Homepage** to uncheck the option.

**8.** Now you can click **Continue** to go to your **email account** or close **Internet Explorer**.

# Conversation

## Paired Conversation

With a partner, take turns reading the A and B parts of the conversation.

| Student A | Hi. What are you doing? |
| --- | --- |
| Student B | I'm writing a message to my friend in India. |
| Student A | Really? How will you send it? |
| Student B | I'll send it to him by email. |
| Student A | Is it easy to send an email all the way to India? |
| Student B | Yes, it is. It's easy to reply, too. |
| Student A | I want to compose and send a question to my doctor, but I don't have email. |
| Student B | Well, you can get a webmail account. |
| Student A | How much does it cost? |
| Student B | Sometimes webmail is free and it is easy to create an account. |
| Student A | Really? Will you help me? |
| Student B | Sure. You need to choose a username you want to use for your account. |
| Student A | Do I need a password? |
| Student B | Yes, you do. |
| Student A | Okay. Now tell me what an Inbox is. |
| Student B | My Inbox is on the screen now. It shows me a list of the email messages that I received. |

# Writing Letters in Microsoft Word

## LEARNING OBJECTIVES

After studying this lesson, you will be able to:

### Computer Objectives

- Use Microsoft Word
- Write personal and business letters
- Use the Word Ribbon
- Check spelling

### Language Objectives

- Use vocabulary words to describe personal and business letters
- Use computer verbs to describe letter writing
- Use computer language to talk about writing letters

*Student Resources labyrinthelab.com/esl3*

# Vocabulary

## Picture Dictionary – Nouns

A noun is the name of a person, place, or thing. The following nouns are introduced in this lesson:

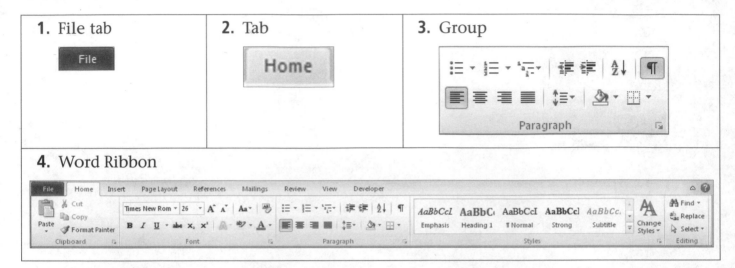

| 1. File tab | 2. Tab | 3. Group |
|---|---|---|

4. Word Ribbon

1. **File tab** – The File tab is different from the other Ribbon tabs; when you click it, you will see the File menu that lets you open, save, and print documents, and do other things

2. **Tab** – A small rectangle on the Word Ribbon that you click to see different groups of buttons

3. **Group** – A set of several buttons that are together in a section under a tab

4. **Word Ribbon** – Made of tabs and buttons grouped together

# Picture Dictionary – Noun (continued)

| 5. Quick Access toolbar | 6. Spelling and Grammar button | 7. ScreenTip | 8. Greeting | 9. Line Spacing button |
|---|---|---|---|---|
|  | ABC | 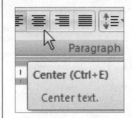 | Dear Maria, My Dear Friend, Dear John, |  |

| 10. Salutation | 11. Closing | 12. Complimentary close |
|---|---|---|
| Dear Ms. Thompson: Dear Governor Simpson: Dear Principal Holtsman: | Sincerely, Fondly, With love and friendship, | Sincerely, Respectfully, With great appreciation, |

5. **Quick Access toolbar** – The bar usually above (but can be below) the Word Ribbon and on the left side; it has buttons that you use often

6. **Spelling and Grammar button** – A special tool that checks your spelling and grammar in a document

7. **ScreenTip** – A little box that appears when you put your mouse on a button (without clicking) on the Ribbon; it gives you information about the button

8. **Greeting** – The opening words for a personal letter

9. **Line Spacing button** – A button in the Paragraph group of the Home tab of the Ribbon that is used to change the space between lines of text

10. **Salutation** – The opening words of a business letter

11. **Closing** – The last words before you sign a personal letter

12. **Complimentary close** – The last words before you sign a business letter

# Computer Verbs

A verb tells an action or what a subject is or does. The following verbs are introduced in this lesson:

| VERB | MEANING | EXAMPLE |
|---|---|---|
| 1. Open (a document) | To put a saved document on the screen | I need to open my document so I can make some changes. |
| 2. Ignore | To pay no attention to something | I know I made a mistake, but I am going to ignore it for now and remember to fix it later. |
| 3. Insert | To put in | Oh, I forgot to type my middle initial. I need to insert it between my first and last names. |
| 4. Format | To make design choices about the way your document looks | Would you please help me format my document so it looks more interesting and professional? |
| 5. Check spelling | To check typed documents to find incorrect spelling and grammar | I have many mistakes in my letter. I will check the spelling now and make the corrections. |
| 6. Zoom | To change the size of the information you see on your screen | I can't read the information. Let me zoom in to make it bigger. |

# Concepts and Exercises

**Microsoft Word**

Microsoft Word is the most frequently used word-processing program in the world. It does much more than WordPad.

---

**HOW TO START MICROSOFT WORD**

Choose Start→All Programs→Microsoft Office→Microsoft Word 2010.

---

You can open Microsoft Word from the Start menu.

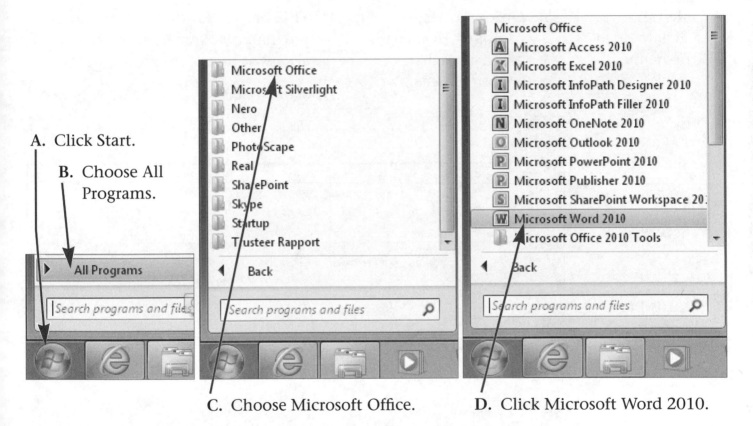

A. Click Start.

B. Choose All Programs.

C. Choose Microsoft Office.

D. Click Microsoft Word 2010.

If you don't see what you are looking for, you may have to scroll up or down.

Word opens on the screen.

**Open Microsoft Word**

In this exercise, you will open Word using the Start menu.

1. Click **Start→All Programs→Microsoft Office→Microsoft Word 2010**.

2. Leave the Word window open.

---

CONCEPT 9.2 **The Word Window**

The pictures below show the parts of the Word 2010 window. Look at the pictures and try to recognize and name each part. These pictures may look a little different from the ones on your screen. If you don't see the Ribbon, double-click the Home tab.

**A. File tab –** Click to open the menu

**B. Quick Access toolbar –** Holds commands that are often used

**C. Title bar –**Tells you the name of the program that you are using (it is always at the top of the window)

**D. Workspace –** Type your work here

**E. Status Bar –** Shows important information

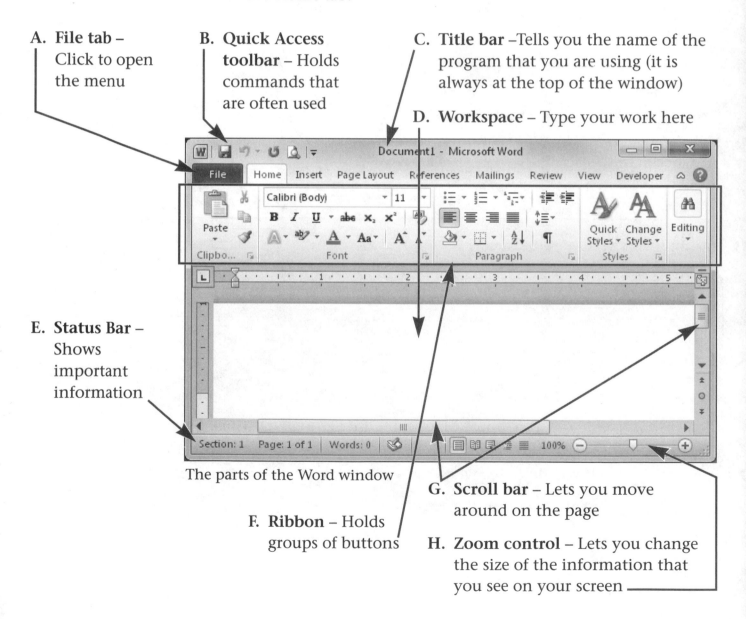

The parts of the Word window

**G. Scroll bar –** Lets you move around on the page

**F. Ribbon –** Holds groups of buttons

**H. Zoom control –** Lets you change the size of the information that you see on your screen

**A. Ribbon tabs** – Click each one to use different groups of buttons

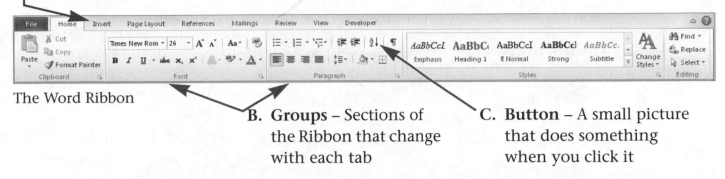

The Word Ribbon

**B. Groups** – Sections of the Ribbon that change with each tab

**C. Button** – A small picture that does something when you click it

The Ribbon helps you create documents and changes how they look. ScreenTips tell you what the Ribbon buttons do.

## The Quick Access Toolbar

The Quick Access toolbar is a special toolbar on the title bar at the top of the window, either above or below the Ribbon. It is easy to use. You can add or remove buttons from this toolbar, so your Quick Access toolbar may have different buttons than what you see here.

**A. Save button** – You click it when you want to save your work.

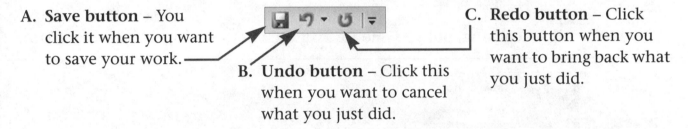

**B. Undo button** – Click this when you want to cancel what you just did.

**C. Redo button** – Click this button when you want to bring back what you just did.

You will learn to use the Undo button in Lesson 10, Copying and Pasting.

## ScreenTips

ScreenTips are little boxes that appear when you place your mouse pointer over each button. Every button has its own ScreenTip describing what happens when you click on it.

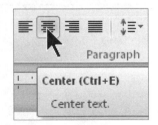

## EXERCISE 9.2  Look at Word's Ribbon

In this exercise, you will learn about the Word Ribbon and its parts.

**1.** Click the **Review** tab on the Word Ribbon near the top of the screen.

**2.** Find (don't click) the **Spelling & Grammar** button.

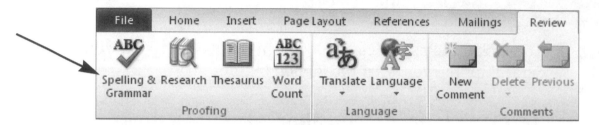

**3.** Click the **Home** tab.

**4.** Without clicking, put your mouse over each button and read the ScreenTips.

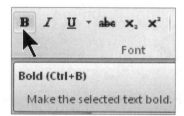

**Typing a Personal Letter**

A personal letter is a letter that you send to a friend or relative. It is not used for business.

**A. Heading** – This part has three lines: the name of the writer, the street address of the writer, and the city, state, and zip code of the writer. There are three blank lines after the heading.

**B. Date** – You should have two empty lines after the date.

**C. Greeting** – You put a comma after the name of the person you are writing to. You must leave an empty line after the greeting.

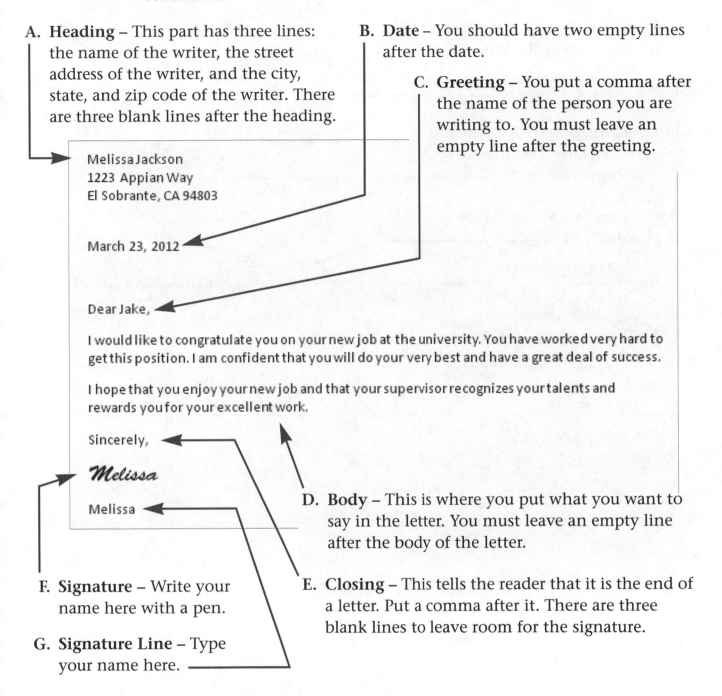

Melissa Jackson
1223 Appian Way
El Sobrante, CA 94803


March 23, 2012


Dear Jake,

I would like to congratulate you on your new job at the university. You have worked very hard to get this position. I am confident that you will do your very best and have a great deal of success.

I hope that you enjoy your new job and that your supervisor recognizes your talents and rewards you for your excellent work.

Sincerely,

*Melissa*

Melissa

**D. Body** – This is where you put what you want to say in the letter. You must leave an empty line after the body of the letter.

**E. Closing** – This tells the reader that it is the end of a letter. Put a comma after it. There are three blank lines to leave room for the signature.

**F. Signature** – Write your name here with a pen.

**G. Signature Line** – Type your name here.

## EXERCISE 9.3 Type a Personal Letter

In this exercise, you will type a personal letter in Word. First you will change the line spacing so your screen matches the pictures in this book.

1. Click the **Line Spacing** menu button on the Home tab of the Word Ribbon. ——

2. Choose the **1.0** option. ——

3. Click the **Line Spacing** menu button again. (Step 2 closed the menu, so now you must reopen it.) ——

4. Choose **Remove Space After Paragraph**. ——

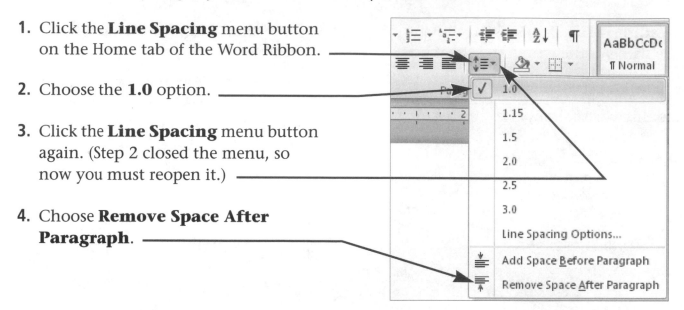

5. Type the personal letter shown below.
   Tap [Enter] to add space between the lines.

   ⚠ **NOTE!** Your letter may not look exactly like the sample on the previous page.

[Enter]
[Enter]
Melissa Jackson [Enter]
1223 Appian Way [Enter]
El Sobrante, CA 94803 [Enter]
[Enter]
[Enter]
March 23, 2012 [Enter]
[Enter]
[Enter]
Dear Jake, [Enter]
[Enter]
I would like to congratulate you on your new job at the
university. You have worked very hard to get this position.
I am confident that you will do your very best and have a
great deal of success. [Enter]
[Enter]
I hope that you enjoy your new job and that your supervisor
recognizes your talents and rewards you for your excellent
work. [Enter]
[Enter]
Sincerely, [Enter]
[Enter]
[Enter]
Melissa [Enter]

6. Click [ File ] →**Save As**.

The Save As dialog box appears, so you can save your letter.

**7.** On the left side, scroll down and click your **USB drive**.

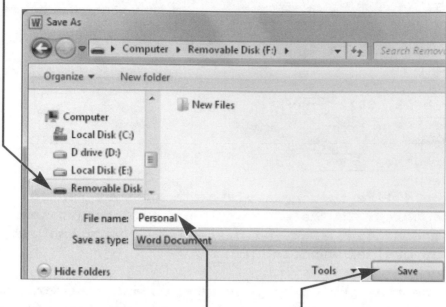

**8.** Type **Personal** as the new filename.

**9.** Click the **Save** button.

**10.** Look at the **title bar**. You should see the filename there.

Leave the file open.

CONCEPT 9.4  **Checking Your Spelling**

Microsoft Word comes with a special tool that will check your spelling and grammar. You will see this button when you click the Review tab of the Word Ribbon.

When you click the Spelling & Grammar button, a dialog box opens. It will show you which words you spelled incorrectly. In this book, we will only discuss spelling changes. You can learn about the grammar changes, underlined in green, in a more advanced Word book.

A. Words not spelled correctly will appear in red.

B. Word will give you some choices of spellings of the word. Click on the one you think is best.

C. Click the Change button if you want to change the word to the one you selected in the Suggestions box.

D. Click Ignore Once if you think the word in the document is spelled correctly.

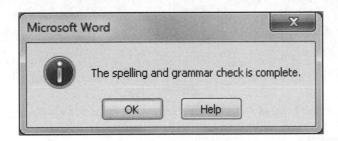

When Word is finished checking the spelling, this box will show.

Click OK. Word also shows you misspelled words as you type. If you see a word with a wavy red underline, it means the word is not spelled correctly or the word is not in Microsoft's dictionary.

Word is finihed

# The Spell Check Feature Is Not Always Correct

Sometimes the spell check feature can make a mistake because it does not know the meaning of words. It would see both of these sentences as correct. But are they both correct?

- I red the book.

- I read the book.

 **EXERCISE 9.4  Check Spelling and Grammar**

In this exercise, you will try the Spelling & Grammar command.

**Before You Begin:** Your document called Personal should still be open for this exercise.

1. Click next to the "l" in "Congratulations" in the first line of the body of the letter.

2. Tap ⬜L on the keyboard so the word is not spelled correctly.

   A red line will appear under the word to tell you that the word is not spelled correctly. Do not pay attention to any other colored lines now. We are only looking at red spelling lines.

3. Click the **Review** tab of the Word Ribbon.

4. Click the **Spelling & Grammar** 🔤 button in the Proofing group on the Review tab.

5. Choose the correct word for any spelling mistakes in your letter.

6. Click the **Ignore Once** button if any green lines for grammar mistakes appear.

   The green grammar lines also show if you have more than one space between words.

7. When you are finished, this box will come up. Click **OK**.

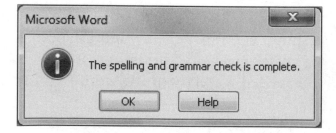

8. Click the **Save** 💾 button on the Quick Access toolbar to save the file.

9. Close the file by clicking ⬛ File →**Close**.

**Typing a Business Letter**

A business letter is different from a personal letter. It is used to communicate with business people. It is often printed on special paper called letterhead that has the business name and address printed at the top.

Here are the parts of a business letter:

**A. Date** – There are four lines inserted on the page before today's date is typed. There are three lines before the inside address. ──▶

**B. Inside address** – This is the name and address of the person receiving the letter. After the address, you must leave an empty line before the salutation.

**C. Salutation** – This part tells who the letter is to. After the person's name, you type a colon (:). After the salutation, you must leave an empty line before the body. ──

**D. Body** – The main part of the letter tells what you want the letter to say. After the body, you must leave an empty line before the closing. ──

November 21, 2012

Ms. Juanita Thompson
Customer Service Representative
Urbana Software
810 Ivanhoe Way
Urbana, IL 61801

Dear Ms. Thompson:

I would like to thank you for the excellent manner in which you assisted me. You were helpful, informative, and very patient. You provided exceptional customer service.

I have already used the software that you recommended. The software has been very helpful in my business. It has saved me a great deal of time and money.

Please send me a list of other software that you carry and would recommend for my business.

Sincerely,

Denise Smith
Small Business Owner

**F. Sender's name** – The name and title of the sender.

**E. Complimentary close** – This comes at the end of the body. The closing is followed by a comma. There are three lines before the sender's name. ──

## Starting a New Document

You start a new document by following the directions below.

**A.** Click the File tab.

**B.** Click New.

**C.** Click Create.

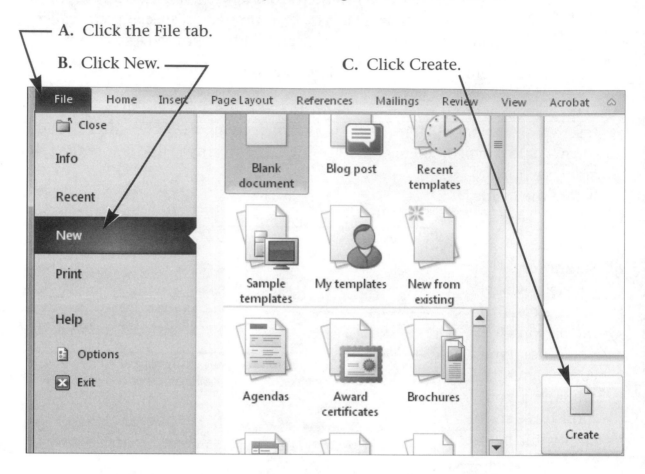

EXERCISE 9.5 **Type a Business Letter**

In this exercise, you will type and then save a business letter.

1. To create a new document, click **File** →**New**→**Create**.
   Word creates a new blank document.

2. Click the **Line Spacing** button and change the spacing to **1.0**. Then, click **Remove Space After Paragraph**.

3. Type this **business letter**. Don't worry if your lines end at different places than in the example.

Enter
Enter
Enter
Enter
**November 21, 2012** Enter
Enter
Enter
Enter
**Ms. Juanita Thompson** Enter
**Customer Service Representative** Enter
**Urbana Software** Enter
**810 Ivanhoe Way** Enter
**Urbana, IL 61801** Enter
Enter
**Dear Ms. Thompson:** Enter
Enter
**I would like to thank you for the excellent manner in which you assisted me. You were helpful, informative, and very patient. You provided exceptional customer service.** Enter
Enter
**I have already used the software that you recommended. The software has been very helpful in my business. It has saved me a great deal of time and money.** Enter
Enter
**Please send me a list of other software that you carry and would recommend for my business.** Enter Enter
**Sincerely,** Enter
Enter
Enter
Enter
**Denise Smith** Enter
**Small Business Owner** Enter

4. Click the **Save** 💾 button on the Quick Access toolbar. Save the file on your **USB drive** as **Business**.

5. Click  File →**Close**.

CONCEPT 9.6 **Opening a Saved File**

You save a file so you can open it later and use it again. This lets you work on the file without needing to retype it.

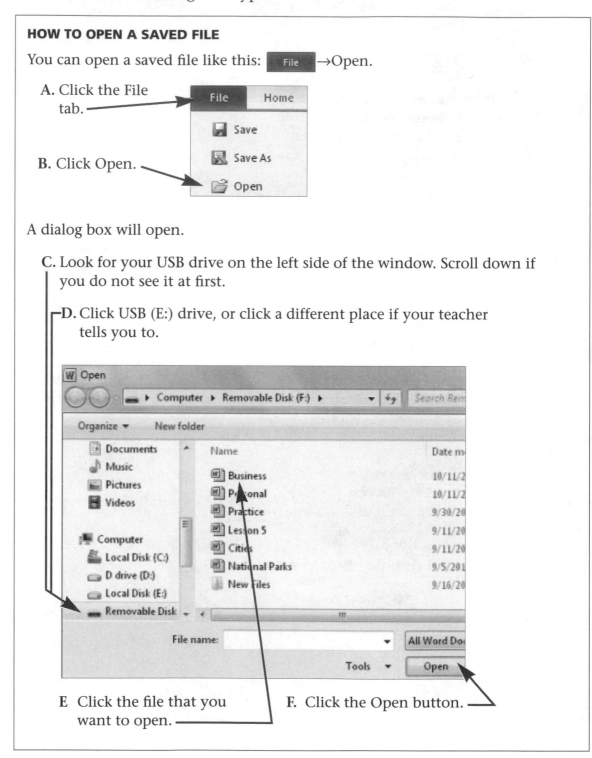

**HOW TO OPEN A SAVED FILE**

You can open a saved file like this: File →Open.

A. Click the File tab.

B. Click Open.

A dialog box will open.

C. Look for your USB drive on the left side of the window. Scroll down if you do not see it at first.

D. Click USB (E:) drive, or click a different place if your teacher tells you to.

E  Click the file that you want to open.

F.  Click the Open button.

## EXERCISE 9.6 Open and Print a File

In this exercise, you will open and print the file that you saved in the last exercise. You will preview the document before you print it.

1. Click **File** →**Open**.

2. Click your **USB drive** on the left side of the window. Scroll down if you do not see it at first.

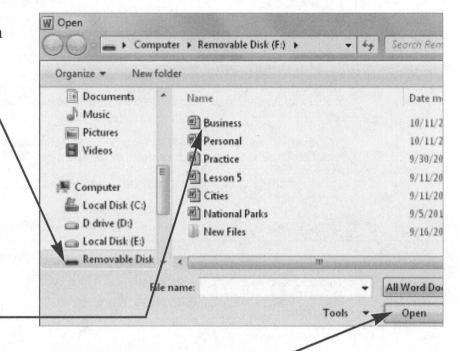

3. Click the **Business** file.

4. Click the **Open** button.
   Your business letter will appear.

**5.** Click  File →**Print** to see how the document will look when you print it.

November 21, 2011

Ms. Juanita Thompson
Customer Service Representative
Urbana Software
810 Ivanhoe Way
Urbana, IL 61801

Dear Ms. Thompson:

I would like to thank you for the excellent manner in which you assisted me. You were helpful, informative, and very patient. You provided exceptional customer service.

I have already used the software that you recommended. The software has been very helpful in my business. It has saved me a great deal of time and money.

Please send me a list of other software that you carry and would recommend for my business.

Sincerely,



Denise Smith
Small Business Owner

**6.** When you are finished looking at the document, click the **Print** button.

**7. Close**  X  Word.

# Skill Builder Exercises

**Type a Personal Letter**

In this exercise, you will type a personal letter.

1. Open Word: **Start→All Programs→Microsoft Office→Microsoft Word 2010**.

2. Type the following **personal letter**:

Enter
Enter
Enter
Samantha Carison Enter
345 Eastern Ave. Enter
Lodi, WI 53555 Enter
Enter
October 20, 2012 Enter
Enter
Enter
Dear Angela, Enter
Enter
We are going to have a health fair at school on Saturday, November 12th at 10 am. I thought that you would like to go, too. You can bring your family. Your family will enjoy it. There will be tests for different diseases, a healthy cooking demonstration, and even fun activities for the children. I know you will have a good time. Enter
Enter
Please call me to let me know if you and your family will be able to go to the health fair. Our telephone number is (209) 555-6642. Try to let me know by Saturday, November 5th so I can get some tickets for you. Enter
Enter
I look forward to seeing you and your family. Please call me so I can tell you more about it. Enter
Enter
Sincerely, Enter
Enter
Enter
Samantha Enter

3. Check the spelling using the **Spelling & Grammar** ☑ button on the Review tab of the Ribbon.

   - Change any words that are not spelled correctly.

   - Do not change any of the names.

4. Click [ File ]→**Save As** and save the file as `Health Fair`.

5. Click [ File ]→**Print**.

   On the left side of the window, Word shows what the document will look like when it prints. Look at your letter carefully before you print it.

6. If you need to change something before you print, click the [ File ] tab to take you out of the Print window to make your changes.

7. When you are ready to print, click the **Print** button inside the Print dialog box.

8. Click [ File ]→**Close**.

---

SKILL BUILDER 9.2    **Type a Business Letter**

In this exercise, you will type and save a business letter. It is an example of a thank-you letter that people should send after a job interview.

1. Click [ File ]→**New**→**Create**.

2. Click the **Line Spacing** ⬍ button and change the spacing to **1.0**. Then, click **Remove Space After Paragraph**.

3. Type this **business letter**:

   `September 5, 2012` [Enter]
   [Enter]
   [Enter]
   [Enter]
   `Mr. Brian Hwang` [Enter]
   `Plumbing Supervisor` [Enter]
   `Expert Plumbing Company` [Enter]
   `1000 Sherwood Place` [Enter]
   `East Brunswick, NJ 08816` [Enter]
   [Enter]
   `Dear Mr. Hwang:` [Enter]
   [Enter]

Thank you for meeting with me to talk about the plumber's job. I appreciated the opportunity to learn more about your company and to talk about my job experience and skills.
`Enter`
`Enter`
I would like to become part of your team. I am very reliable and will work hard to do a good job. One of my best qualities is my excellent customer service. I hope to hear from you soon. `Enter`
`Enter`
Thank you for taking the time to interview me. `Enter`
`Enter`
Sincerely, `Enter`
`Enter`
`Enter`
`Enter`
Salil Chauhan `Enter`

4. Check the spelling using the **Spelling & Grammar** 🗹 button on the Review tab of the Ribbon.

   - Decide whether to change or ignore what is shown in the dialog box.

   - Change any words that are not spelled correctly.

   - Do not change any of the names.

5. Click `File` →**Save As** and save the file as `Interview Thank You Letter`.

6. Click `File` →**Print**.

   On the left side of the window, Word shows what the document will look like when it prints. Look at your letter carefully before you print it.

7. If you need to change something before you print, click the `File` tab to take you out of the Print window to make your changes.

8. When you are ready to print, click the **Print** button inside the Print dialog box.

9. Click `File` →**Close**.

**Edit a Letter**

In this exercise, you will make changes to your saved Health Fair letter.

1. Click [File] →**Open**. Open the **Health Fair** letter you created in Skill Builder 9.1.

2. Make the changes shown in the next picture. Delete the words that are crossed out and add the written words.

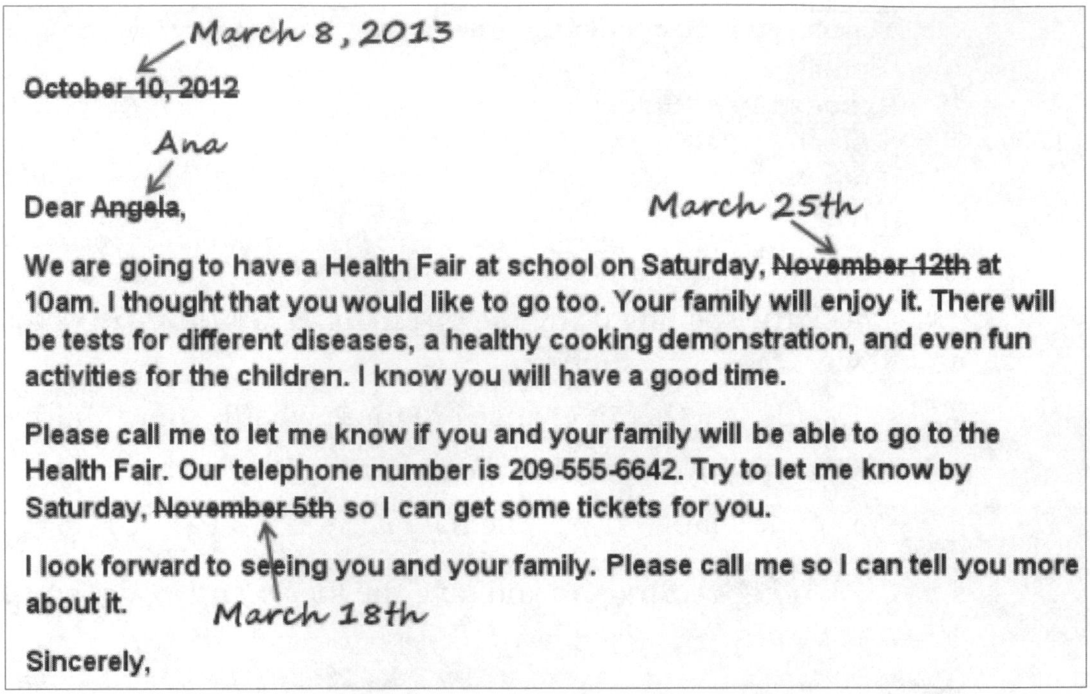

3. Click [File] →**Save As** and save the file as **Health Fair 2**.

4. **Print** the document.

5. Click [File] →**Close**.

**Personal Project: Type a Personal Letter**

In this exercise, you will type and save your own personal letter.

1. Type a personal letter to a friend telling him or her about a new job that you will start soon.

2. When you finish typing, **save** the letter with the name **New Job**.

3. **Print** and then **close** the letter.

---

**Personal Project: Type a Business Letter**

In this exercise, you will type and save your own business letter.

1. Type a business letter to your electric company. (Their address should be on your electric bill.) Explain that there is a street light that does not work in front of your house. Ask them to fix the street light.

2. When you finish typing, **save** the letter with the name **Street Light**.

3. **Print** and then **close** the letter.

---

# Conversation

## Paired Conversation

With a partner, take turns reading the A and B parts of the conversation.

| | |
|---|---|
| Student A | Hi! What's the matter? |
| Student B | I'm having trouble writing a letter to my grandma in Microsoft Word. |
| Student A | Why are you having trouble? |
| Student B | Well, I can't think of a good greeting. |
| Student A | How about "My Dearest Grandma"? |
| Student B | That sounds good! |
| Student A | Well, you don't want it to sound like a business letter! |
| Student B | That's true! Personal letters are less formal. |
| Student A | You should format your letter so it will look nice. |
| Student B | I know. I want a nice font and bigger letters so my grandmother can read it easily. |
| Student A | You will need to use the Word Ribbon. |
| Student B | I only know a little bit about the Ribbon with all the groups of buttons. |
| Student A | Don't worry! If you read the ScreenTips, they will help you to select the changes you need to format your text. |
| Student B | Yes, they are very helpful. |
| Student A | Have you thought about a closing? |
| Student B | I think I will write "Your Loving Granddaughter". |
| Student A | That sounds great. Don't forget to check your spelling! |
| Student B | I won't! I'll print it and send it to her today. |

# Copying and Pasting

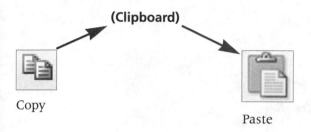

(Clipboard)

Copy

Paste

## LEARNING OBJECTIVES

After studying this lesson, you will be able to:

**Computer Objectives**

- Use Undo
- Use Copy and Paste
- Move from one open program to another
- Create a simple résumé

**Language Objectives**

- Use vocabulary words to describe how to copy and paste
- Use computer verbs to describe drag and drop, and undo actions
- Explain the parts of a simple résumé to a partner
- Talk with a partner about how to copy and paste

*Student Resources labyrinthelab.com/esl3*

# Picture Dictionary – Nouns

A noun is the name of a person, place, or thing. The following nouns are introduced in this lesson:

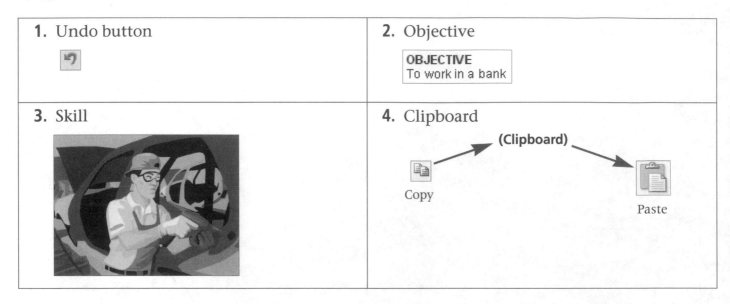

| | |
|---|---|
| **1.** Undo button | **2.** Objective |
| **3.** Skill | **4.** Clipboard |

1. **Undo button** – A button that allows you to cancel the last thing you did

2. **Objective** – The kind of job or goal that someone wants

3. **Skill** – Something you can do that requires learning and practice

4. **Clipboard** – The place in the computer's memory where something goes when you copy it and before you paste it in a new location

# Picture Dictionary – Nouns (continued)

| | |
|---|---|
| **5.** Location<br> | **6.** Result<br><br>**Before:** Learning English is fun.<br><br>**After: Learning English is fun.** |

**7.** Clipboard group (on the Word Ribbon)

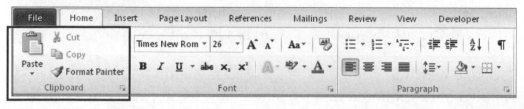

**5. Location** – The place where something is

**6. Result** – The effect of a change you make

**7. Clipboard group** – Part of the Home tab of the Word Ribbon that holds the Cut, Copy, and Paste buttons

# Computer Verbs

A verb tells an action what a subject is or does. The following verbs are introduced in this lesson:

| VERB | MEANING | EXAMPLE |
|------|---------|---------|
| **1.** Cut | To take away or delete text or information you do not want | I don't like that sentence there. I am going to cut it from the first paragraph and paste it in the last paragraph. |
| **2.** Copy | To duplicate text in a document so you can put it in a different location | I will copy this sentence from Mr. Smith's letter so I can put it in Mr. Garcia's letter, too. |
| **3.** Paste | To take text that you copied and put it in a new location | I copied my address from the first letter. Now I will paste it into all of the other letters. |
| **4.** Move | To change the location of text or other information | My address is in the wrong place. I will move it so it is under my name. |
| **5.** Undo | To cancel the last thing you did | Oops, I made a mistake. I will press the Undo button to cancel it. |
| **6.** Multitask | To do more than one thing at the same time | I multitask when I cook and talk on the telephone at the same time. |

**!NOTE!** When you cut something in the computer, it stays in the memory so you can paste it somewhere else. When you delete something, you cannot paste it. You can undo both cut and delete actions.

# Concepts and Exercises

CONCEPT 10.1 **Typing a Résumé**

A résumé is a special document that you can use to help you find a job. It should have important information that tells people why they should give you a job. Look at the parts of a résumé below.

**A.** Put your name, address, phone number, and email address here.

**Juan Garcia**
*725 Lone Star Way*
*Del Rio, Texas 78840*
**(830) 775-1586**
jgarciatx@yahoo.com

**OBJECTIVE**

Seeking a bank teller position in San Antonio

**B.** Explain the kind of job you want here.

**WORK EXPERIENCE**

**Bank Teller** – Lake Amistad Bank, Del Rio, TX
2007-Present
- Support customers in all types of banking transactions
- Assist in all clerical responsibilities within the bank
- Promoted because of accuracy, speed, and other skills
- Responsible for cash/checking deposits, processing loan payments, opening and getting direct deposits accounts

**C.** List the jobs you have had in the past. It is important to include the years, but you do not have to list all of the places you have worked.

**ADDITIONAL SKILLS**

- Accurate data entry
- Experience with Microsoft Word, Internet, and email
- Experience with handling money
- Fluent in Spanish and English

**D.** Put important skills you want the employer to notice here.

**AWARDS**
- July 2009 – Teller of the Month
- December 2011 – Excellent Customer Service Award

**EDUCATION**

**San Felipe High School**, Del Rio, TX, Date of Graduation: June 7, 2006
**Rio Grande College**, Accounting classes 2006-2009

**E.** List any special recognition that was given to you to show that you are a good worker.

**F.** List your high school, college, or other training.

**EXERCISE 10.1** **Type and Format a Résumé**

In this exercise, you will type a résumé and then format it to make it look more professional.

1. Open Word: **Start→All Programs→Microsoft Office→Microsoft Word 2010**.

2. Click the **Line Spacing** [≡▼] button and change the spacing to **1.0**. Then, click **Remove Space After Paragraph**.

   If you need help, look at Exercise 9.3.

3. Type the following **résumé**. To make the line below the personal information, hold down [Shift] and tap [-] until the line is complete. If your line is too long, use [Backspace] until the line is the right size.

   You must use the text formatting that you learned in Lesson 5, Doing More with WordPad. Go back and review how to use the alignment, bold, and bullets buttons.

**Juan Garcia**
*725 Lone Star Way*
*Del Rio, Texas 78840*
(830) 775-1586
jgarciatx@yahoo.com

## OBJECTIVE

Seeking a bank teller position in San Antonio

## WORK EXPERIENCE

**Bank Teller** – Lake Amistad Bank, Del Rio, TX
2007-Present
- Support customers in all types of banking transactions
- Assist in all clerical responsibilities within the bank
- Promoted because of accuracy, speed, and other skills
- Responsible for cash/checking deposits, processing loan payments, opening accounts, and getting direct deposits accounts

## ADDITIONAL SKILLS

- Accurate data entry
- Experience with Microsoft Word, Internet, and email
- Experience with handling money
- Fluent in Spanish and English

## AWARDS
- July 2009 – Teller of the Month
- December 2011 – Excellent Customer Service Award

## EDUCATION

**San Felipe High School**, Del Rio, TX, Date of Graduation: June 7, 2006
**Rio Grande College**, Accounting classes 2006-2009

---

**4. Save** the file as **Practice Resume** and then **close** it.

You will be doing more work with résumés later in this lesson.

---

**Copying and Pasting within a Program**

Sometimes you want to repeat a word or sentence in a document. To save time, you can copy that information instead of typing it again. When you copy something, it goes to a place in the computer's memory that you cannot see, called the Clipboard. The computer keeps it there until you copy something else or close the program.

## An Example of Copy and Paste

These figures show how the Copy and Paste commands work.

**A.** Select (highlight) what you want to copy and then click the Copy button.

> Melissa Jackson
> 1223 Appian Way
> El Sobrante, CA 94803
>
> October 23, 2009
>
> Dear Jake,
>
> I would like to congratulate you on your new job at the university. You have worked very hard to get this position. I am confident that you will do your very best and have a great deal of success.
>
> I hope that you enjoy your new job and that your supervisor recognizes your talents and rewards you for your excellent work.

**B.** You click where you want to paste what you copied.

> I would like to congratulate you on your new job at the university. You have worked very hard to get this position. I am confident that you will do your very best and have a great deal of success.
>
> I hope that you enjoy your new job and that your supervisor recognizes your talents and rewards you for your excellent work. We look forward to seeing you at the family picnic in |

**C.** After you click the Paste button, the copied text appears.

> I hope that you enjoy your new job and that your supervisor recognizes your talents and rewards you for your excellent work. We look forward to seeing you at the family picnic in El Sobrante.

A. To copy information, you must highlight it first.

B. Click the Copy  button on the Home tab in the Clipboard group of the Word Ribbon. You will not see anything happen yet. The information is now in a place in the computer called the Clipboard.

C. Click where you want the information to go.

D. Click the Paste  button in the Clipboard group on the Home tab of the Word Ribbon to put the information into your document.

E. If you see any other buttons appear automatically, do not click on them. They will go away as you do more work or after you save the file.

F. The pasted information stays where it was and it also goes to the new location.

## EXERCISE 10.2   Open and Change a Letter File

In this exercise, you will open, change, and save a personal letter in Word.

1. Open Word: **Start→All Programs→Microsoft Office→Microsoft Word 2010**.

2. Click ▮ File ▮ →**Open**. Click the **Personal** file you made in the last lesson and then click **Open**.

3. Highlight "El Sobrante" near the top of the letter.

> Melissa Jackson
> 1223 Appian Way
> El Sobrante, CA 94803

4. Click the **Copy**  button on the Home tab of the Word Ribbon.

5. Click at the end of the last paragraph in the body of the letter.

> I would like to congratulate you on your new job at the university. You have worked very hard to get this position. I am confident that you will do your very best and have a great deal of success.
>
> I hope that you enjoy your new job and that your supervisor recognizes your talents and rewards you for your excellent work.|
>
> Sincerely,

6. Put in a space then type the following:

**We look forward to seeing you at the family picnic in**

## Paste the Copied Address

7. Put in another space by tapping [Spacebar]. Then, click the **Paste** button to paste "El Sobrante" at the end of the sentence you just typed.

8. Type a period to end the sentence. The changed paragraph should look like this:

> I hope that you enjoy your new job and that your supervisor recognizes your talents and rewards you for your excellent work. We look forward to seeing you at the family picnic in El Sobrante.
>
> Sincerely,

Word pastes the copied text into the new position. Do not close this document.

---

CONCEPT 10.3   **Saving a File with a New Name**

Sometimes you want to make changes to a file but still keep the old unchanged file. You can keep the old file under the old name and save the new file with the changes using a new name.

---

**HOW TO SAVE A FILE WITH A NEW NAME**

A. Open the file.

B. Make the changes that you want to make.

C. Save the changed file using File →Save As.

D. If you want to change the location, use the navigation pane on the left and click the new place where you want to save your file (or double-click it on the right side of the Save As box).

E. Type a new name for the file in the File Name box.

F. Click the Save button.

---

**EXERCISE 10.3** **Change the Filename of a Letter**

In this exercise, you will make changes to the Personal document and save it with a different filename. This way you will keep the old file and have the new one, too.

**1.** Highlight Melissa's name and address at the top of the letter.

Melissa Jackson
1223 Appian Way
El Sobrante, CA 94803

**2.** Press [Delete] to remove the highlighted area.

**3.** Click [ File ] →**Save As** and name the file as **Personal2**.

**4.** Click [ File ] →**Close**.

---

**CONCEPT 10.4** **Using Undo**

You use Undo to cancel the last thing you did. If you just deleted a word and you want to bring it back, you want to undo the delete.

This is the button on the Quick Access Toolbar that you click to undo.

**EXERCISE 10.4** **Use Cut and Undo**

In this exercise, you will open the Business file from Lesson 9 and use Cut and Undo. When you use Cut, the information stays in the memory so you can paste it somewhere else if you want.

1. Click [ File ] →**Open** and open your **Business** file.

2. Highlight the first sentence in the body of the letter.

> Dear Ms. Thompson:
>
> I would like to thank you for the excellent manner in which you assisted me. Y
> were helpful, informative, and very patient. You provided exceptional custome

3. Click the **Cut** ✂ button in the Clipboard group.

   The highlighted sentence disappears.

4. Click the **Undo** ↺ button.

   The sentence appears again.

5. Click in the first line of the complimentary close between "Sincerely" and the comma.

   Sincerely

6. Type a space and the word **Yours**.

7. Click the **Undo** ↺ button.

   The word that you just typed disappears.

8. Save the file as **Business2**. Do not close it.

CONCEPT 10.5 **Moving Text in Word**

The easiest way to move text is to highlight it and then drag it to a new place. It is different from copy and paste because the text does not stay where it was before. It is moved only to the new place. This is how it is done.

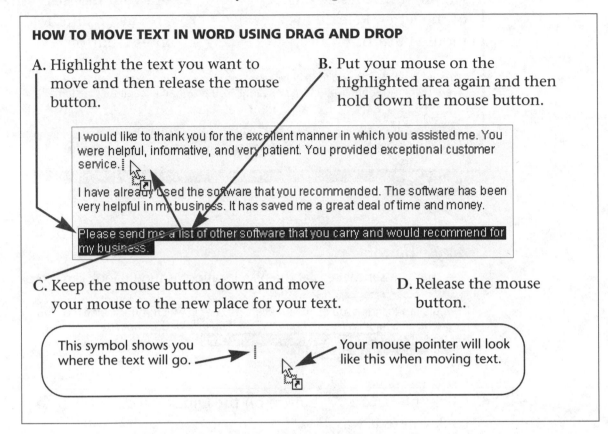

**HOW TO MOVE TEXT IN WORD USING DRAG AND DROP**

A. Highlight the text you want to move and then release the mouse button.

B. Put your mouse on the highlighted area again and then hold down the mouse button.

> I would like to thank you for the excellent manner in which you assisted me. You were helpful, informative, and very patient. You provided exceptional customer service.
>
> I have already used the software that you recommended. The software has been very helpful in my business. It has saved me a great deal of time and money.
>
> Please send me a list of other software that you carry and would recommend for my business.

C. Keep the mouse button down and move your mouse to the new place for your text.

D. Release the mouse button.

This symbol shows you where the text will go. → ⋮

Your mouse pointer will look like this when moving text.

**EXERCISE 10.5** **Move Text with Drag and Drop**

In this exercise, you will move the last sentence up to the first paragraph and then undo the action.

**1.** Highlight the last sentence of the letter. Release the mouse button.

**2.** Put your mouse on the highlighted area again and hold down the mouse button.

> I would like to thank you for the excellent manner in which you assisted me. You were helpful, informative, and very patient. You provided exceptional customer service.
>
> I have already used the software that you recommended. The software has been very helpful in my business. It has saved me a great deal of time and money.
>
> Please send me a list of other software that you carry and would recommend for my business.

**3.** Drag the sentence to the end of the first paragraph of the letter. Release the mouse button.

See that the sentence is at the new location. It should look like the picture below:

> I would like to thank you for the excellent manner in which you assisted me. You were helpful, informative, and very patient. You provided exceptional customer service. Please send me a list of other software that you carry and would recommend for my business.

**4.** Click the **Undo** button on the Quick Access toolbar to put the sentence back where it was.

**5.** Click **File** →**Close**.

**6.** Choose **No** if asked whether you want to save your changes.

**Using Right-Click to Copy and Paste**

Sometimes it is easier to copy and paste by clicking the right mouse button.

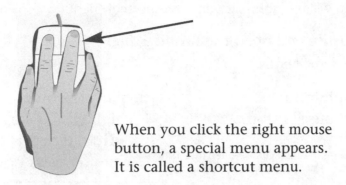

When you click the right mouse button, a special menu appears. It is called a shortcut menu.

---

**HOW TO COPY USING A RIGHT-CLICK AND THE SHORTCUT MENU**

A. Holding down the left mouse button, highlight what you want to copy.

B. Release the left button, and then press down the right button in the highlighted area and release it. The shortcut menu will appear.

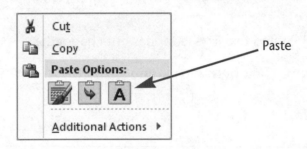

C. Click Copy with the left mouse button.

D. Click where you want the information to go in the document you are in or in a different one.

E. Right-click to show the shortcut menu.

F. With the left button, click Paste. (Or, you can use the Paste button on the Home tab of the Ribbon.)

---

EXERCISE 10.6 **Copy Text with Right-Click**

In this exercise, you will use right-click and the shortcut menu to copy and paste text.

1. Click File →**Open** and open the Business file.

   Now you will copy some text.

2. Highlight the second paragraph in the body of the letter. Release the left mouse button.

3. Put your mouse on the highlighted area and **right-click**. (See that the shortcut menu shows now.)

4. Click **Copy** with the left mouse button.

   Word copies the highlighted text The letter has not changed.

5. With the left button, click below the date near the top of the letter.

November 21, 2012

Ms. Juanita Thompson
Customer Service Representative
Urbana Software
810 Ivanhoe Way
Urbana, IL 61801

6. **Right-click** in the same place to bring up the shortcut menu. Click **Paste** with the left button.

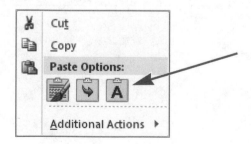

   Now you will see the sentence copied below the date, as in the following figure.

November 21, 2012
I have already used the software that you recommended. The software has been very helpful in my business. It has saved me a great deal of time and money.

**7.** Highlight the sentences you just pasted below the date and press [Delete].

**8.** Save 💾 the Business file.

**9.** Click [ File ]→**Close**.
Word closes the document but leaves the Word program open.

**10.** Click [ File ]→**New**→**Create**.
Word creates a new blank document for the next exercise.

---

CONCEPT 10.7 **Copying from One Program to Another**

You have more choices with the documents you make if you can copy information from one program and paste it into another. You can copy pictures and text.

> **HOW TO COPY FROM ONE PROGRAM AND PASTE INTO ANOTHER**
>
> **A.** Open one of the programs.
>
> **B.** Find and select what you want to copy.
>
> **C.** Click the Copy 📋 button (or use Edit→Copy from the menu if you do not see a Copy button).
>
> **D.** Open the program you want to copy to. At this point, you will have both of the programs open. (This is called multitasking.)
>
> **E.** Click where you want the information to go.
>
> **F.** Click the Paste 📋 (or use Edit→Paste from the menu if you do not see a Paste button).

**EXERCISE 10.7** **Copy from the Calculator into Word**

In this exercise, you will do a calculation on the Calculator program, copy the answer, and paste the answer into Word.

1.  Open the Calculator: **Start→All Programs→Accessories→Calculator**.

2.  Follow these steps to multiply 56 by 10:

    **A.** Click the **5 button** and then the **6 button**. You can see the number appear in the number box near the top of the calculator.

    **B.** Click the **multiplication (*) sign**.

    **C.** Click the **1 button** and then the **0 button**.

    **D.** Click the **equal (=) sign** to finish.

    You can see the answer (560) in the number box.

3.  Click **Edit→Copy** from the menu bar.

    You cannot use the Copy button because the calculator does not have one.

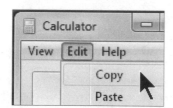

4.  Click the **Microsoft Word** button on the Windows taskbar at the bottom of the screen. (The new blank document that you made at the end of the last exercise should be open.)

5.  Type this sentence: `My answer from the calculator is`

6.  Click the **Paste** button, and then type a period at the end of the sentence.

    Your result should look like this: *My answer from the calculator is 560.*

7.  **Save** the file as **Answer**.

8.  **Close** ▬X▬ the Word program.

    Use the Close button on the Word title bar.

9.  **Close** ▬X▬ the Calculator program.

# Skill Builder Exercises

**SKILL BUILDER 10.1** ## Move Text by Dragging

In this exercise, you will open a file and then move text in it using drag and drop.

1. Open Word: **Start→All Programs→Microsoft Office→Microsoft Word 2010**.

2. Click [ File ] **→Open** and open the **Practice Resume** file from Exercise 10.1.

3. Highlight the EDUCATION section the line of space below it and then release the mouse button.

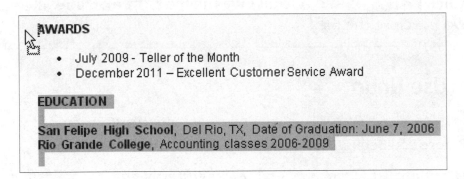

4. Move your mouse onto the highlighted area and hold down the left mouse button.

5. Keep the mouse button down and drag until you see a small dashed line in front of AWARDS. Release the mouse button.

**6.** After you have moved the paragraph, the letter should look like this:

---

**ADDITIONAL SKILLS**

- Accurate data entry
- Experience with Microsoft Word, Internet, and email
- Experience with handling money
- Fluent in Spanish and English

**EDUCATION**

**San Felipe High School**, Del Rio, TX, Date of Graduation: June 7, 2006
**Rio Grande College**, Accounting classes 2006-2009

**AWARDS**

- July 2009 – Teller of the Month
- December 2011 – Excellent Customer Service Award

---

**7.** Click [ File ] →**Save As** and save the file as **Practice Resume 2**. Do *not* close the file.

---

SKILL BUILDER 10.2 **Use Undo**

In this exercise, you will use the Undo button to reverse changes to your document.
**Before You Begin**: The Practice Resume 2 file should still be open.

**1.** Highlight all of the personal information section at the top of the document.

**2.** Click the **Cut** [✂] button in the Clipboard group to remove it.

**3.** Click the **Undo** [↺] button to bring it back.

**4.** Highlight Juan's telephone number in the personal information section and type your phone number to replace it.

**5.** Click the **Undo** [↺] button to change it back.

**6.** **Close** [ X ] Word. If a message appears asking if you want to save the file, click **No**.

---

**Copy a Picture from the Internet into Word**

In this exercise, you will find a picture to copy. Then you will copy it and paste it into Word.

1. Open **Internet Explorer**. If you are not at Google's web page, click once in the **address bar**, type **google.com**, and press Enter.

2. Click the **Images** link.

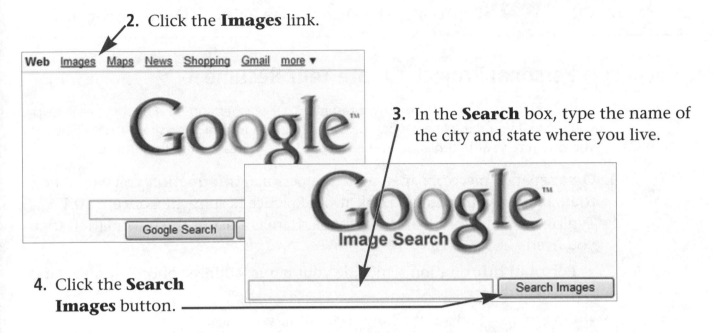

3. In the **Search** box, type the name of the city and state where you live.

4. Click the **Search Images** button.

Google displays pictures found by your search. Now you will copy a picture.

5. Look at the pictures from the search results. Click on one picture you like.

Google displays the small picture at the top of the page. You may also see a larger picture below the small one.

6. **Right-click** on the picture at the top of the page. (You will see a shortcut menu.)

Open link
Open link in new tab
Open link in new window
Save target as...
Print target

Show picture
Save picture as...
E-mail picture...
Print picture...
Go to My Pictures
Set as background

Cut
Copy
Copy shortcut
Paste

7. Left-click **Copy** on the shortcut menu.

8. Open **Word**, type the name of your city, and press [Enter].

9. Type **four sentences** about the city or area where you live.

10. Click the **Paste** 📋 button on the Home tab in the Clipboard group.

11. **Save** 💾 your file as `My City`.

12. Click [File] →**Print**→**Print**. When you are finished, **close** the window.

---

SKILL BUILDER 10.4 **Personal Project: Create Your Résumé**

In this exercise, you create your own résumé. Your teacher and other students will help you if you if you don't know what to write. There is a résumé worksheet that will help you organize your information in the workbook that goes with this textbook.

1. On a separate piece of paper, write the personal information you would like to include in your résumé. Look at the Practice Resume in Concept 10.1, Typing a Résumé or in your workbook. Here is a list of the information that you need:

   - **Personal information** – Include your name, address, phone number, and email address.

   - **Objective** – Explain the kind of job that you want.

   - **Work Experience** – List jobs you have had in the past related to the position you are applying for. It is important to include the years and begin with the most recent or present job (It is not necessary to put in all of the places that you worked.)

   - **Additional Skills** – List important skills that you want the employer to notice.

   - **Awards** – List special things that were given to you to show that you were a good worker. If you do not have any awards, you do not need this part.

   - **Education** – Include any high school, college, or training related to this position.

2. Open Word: **Start→All Programs→Microsoft Office→Microsoft Word 2010**.

3. Click the **Line Spacing** button and change the spacing to **1.0**. Then, click **Remove Space After Paragraph**.

4. Type your personal information centered so it looks like the sample résumé.

5. Hold down [Shift] and tap [-] to make a line underneath your personal information.

6. Type your **Objective**, **Work Experience**, **Additional Skills**, **Awards**, and **Education** sections into Word.

7. Read over your work carefully. Make any changes and corrections.

8. **Save** your résumé to your **USB drive** using your name as the filename.

9. **Print** your résumé and then read it again to check it. Have someone else read it and tell you what they think about it.

10. Make any changes that you need to make and then save your résumé again. If you made changes, print the file again.

11. When you are finished, **close all windows**.

---

SKILL BUILDER 10.5  **Personal Project: Make a Document about an Emergency Vehicle**

In this exercise, you will create a Word document about an emergency vehicle. First you will find a picture, copy it, and paste it into your Word document. Below the picture, you will type some information about the emergency vehicle. Then you will save and print the document.

1. Use **Google** to find a picture of a police car, a fire truck, or an ambulance.

2. **Copy** the picture into Word. Press [→] on the keyboard and then press [Enter] to get to the next line under the picture.

3. Type the name of the emergency vehicle you copied and press [Enter].

4. Type **one paragraph** that tells about the kinds of emergencies that vehicle is used for.

5. **Save** 💾 the file on your USB drive as Emergency.

6. Click [ File ] →**Print**→**Print**.

7. **Close** [ X ] Word.

---

 # Conversation

## Paired Conversation

With a partner, take turns reading the A and B parts of the conversation.

| | |
|---|---|
| Student A | Greetings, my friend! |
| Student B | Hi! Are you ready for our computer lesson today? |
| Student A | Yes. I have so many files that I need to work on. |
| Student B | That's great. We can multitask today. |
| Student A | What's multitasking? |
| Student B | It means working with two or more programs at the same time. |
| Student A | Oh, that's a good word. Is task a word that means a job that you need to do? |
| Student B | Yes. Today we will learn how to copy to the Clipboard. |
| Student A | And then we will paste the information somewhere else, right? |
| Student B | That's right. We'll also learn how to cut text and move it. |
| Student A | I really need to learn how to cut and move text! |
| Student B | Cut, copy, and paste are all on the Clipboard group. |
| Student A | Is the Clipboard group on the Word Ribbon? |
| Student B | Yes! You seem to understand this stuff. |
| Student A | Thanks. I know the location of the files I want to work on. |
| Student B | Good. When you finish, make sure to save your new file to your USB drive and to type a filename in the File Name box. |
| Student A | Great! I'll remember where I saved it. |
| Student B | You're learning so quickly. Soon you can use these skills to search for a job. |

# Notes

# Notes

# Notes

# Notes

# Notes

# Notes

# Notes

# Notes